FOUNDATIONS OF MODERN PSYCHOLOGY SERIES

Richard S. Lazarus, Editor

The Psychological Development of the Child, 2nd ed.,   Paul Mussen

Tests and Measurements, 2nd ed.,   Leona E. Tyler

Motivation and Emotion,   Edward J. Murray

Personality, 2nd ed.,   Richard S. Lazarus

Clinical Psychology,   Julian B. Rotter

Sensory Psychology,   Conrad G. Mueller

Perception, 2nd ed.,   Julian E. Hochberg

Learning, 2nd ed.,   Sarnoff A. Mednick, Howard R. Pollio,
and Elizabeth F. Loftus

Language and Thought,   John B. Carroll

Social Psychology, 2nd ed.,   William W. Lambert and Wallace E. Lambert

Physiological Psychology,   Philip Teitelbaum

Educational Psychology,   Donald Ross Green

The Nature of Psychological Inquiry,   Ray Hyman

Organizational Psychology, 2nd ed.,   Edgar H. Schein

Abnormal Psychology,   Sheldon Cashdan

Humanistic Psychology,   John Shaffer

H.

PAUL MUSSEN

Professor of Psychology
Director, Institute of Human Development
University of California, Berkeley

second edition

The Psychological Development of the Child

of the Child

PRENTICE-HALL, INC., ENGLEWOOD CLIFFS, NEW JERSEY

Library of Congress Cataloging in Publication Data

MUSSEN, PAUL HENRY.
   The psychological development of the child.

   (Foundations of modern psychology series)
   Includes bibliographical references.
   1. Child study. I. Title.
BF721.M89 1973   155.4   73-791 ✓
ISBN 0-13-732321-2
ISBN 0-13-732313-1 (pbk.)

© *1973, 1963 by*

Prentice-Hall, Inc., Englewood Cliffs, N.J.

10   9   8   7   6   5   4   3   2   1

Prentice-Hall International, Inc., London

Prentice-Hall of Australia, Pty. Ltd., Sydney

Prentice-Hall of Canada, Ltd., Toronto

Prentice-Hall of India Private Limited, New Delhi

Prentice-Hall of Japan, Inc., Tokyo

To Ethel, Michele, and Jimmy

Contents

THREE
Language, Cognitive Development, and Intelligence *26*

THE CHILD'S THOUGHT

THE DEVELOPMENT OF INTELLIGENCE

FOUR
Personality Development

I: BIOLOGICAL AND CULTURAL INFLUENCES *47*

BIOLOGICAL FACTORS

SOCIALIZATION AND CULTURAL INFLUENCES ON PERSONALITY

FIVE
Personality Development

II: FAMILIAL, PEER, AND SITUATIONAL INFLUENCES *60*

PEERS AS AGENTS OF SOCIALIZATION

STABILITY OF PERSONALITY CHARACTERISTICS

SITUATIONAL DETERMINANTS OF BEHAVIOR

THE MODIFICATION OF CHILDREN'S PERSONALITY CHARACTERISTICS

SIX
The Development of Social Behavior *90*

SOCIAL BEHAVIOR DURING THE PRESCHOOL YEARS

SOCIAL RELATIONSHIPS IN MIDDLE CHILDHOOD

SOCIAL PATTERNS OF ADOLESCENTS

DEVELOPMENTAL PSYCHOLOGY AND HUMAN WELFARE

Foundations of
Modern Psychology Series

The tremendous growth and vitality of psychology and its increasing fusion with the social and biological sciences demand a search for new approaches to teaching at the introductory level. We can no longer feel content with the traditional basic course, geared as it usually is to a single text that tries to skim everything, that sacrifices depth for breadth. Psychology has become too diverse for any one person, or group, to write about with complete authority. The alternative, a book that ignores many essential areas in order to present more comprehensively and effectively a particular aspect or view of psychology, is also insufficient, for in this solution many key areas are simply not communicated to the student at all.

The Foundations of Modern Psychology Series was the first in what has become a growing trend in psychology toward groups of short texts dealing with various basic subjects, each written by an active authority. It was conceived with the idea of providing greater flexibility for instructors teaching general courses than was ordinarily available in the large, encyclopedic textbooks, and greater depth of presentation for individual topics not typically given much space in introductory textbooks.

The earliest volumes appeared in 1963, the latest not until 1973. Well over one and a quarter million copies, collectively, have been sold, attesting to the widespread use of these books in the teaching of psychology. Individual volumes have been used as supplementary texts, or as *the* text, in various undergraduate courses in psychology, education, public health, and sociology, and clusters of volumes have served as the text in beginning undergraduate courses in general psychology. Groups of volumes have been translated into eight languages, including Dutch, Hebrew, Italian, Japanese, Polish, Portuguese, Spanish, and Swedish.

With wide variation in publication date and type of content, some of the volumes need revision, while others do not. We have left this decision to the individual author who best knows his book in relation to the state of the field. Some will remain unchanged, some will be modestly changed, and still others completely rewritten. In the new series edition, we have also opted for some variation in the length and style of individual books, to reflect the different ways in which they have been used as texts.

There has never been stronger interest in good teaching in our colleges and universities than there is now; and for this the availability of high quality, well-written, and stimulating text materials highlighting the exciting and continuing search for knowledge is a prime prerequisite. This is especially the case in undergraduate courses where large numbers of students must have access to suitable readings. The Foundations of Modern Psychology Series represents our ongoing attempt to provide college teachers with the best textbook materials we can create.

Richard S. Lazarus, Editor

Preface

The first edition of this book was published ten years ago. The field of developmental psychology has changed radically in the interim years; consequently, the earlier edition has been completely revised to reflect the major changes. These include: increased research emphasis on cognition, especially the work of Piaget; the effects of early environmental stimulation on later cognitive functioning and the related issue of compensatory education; systematic investigations of the capabilities of infants; the development of both syntactic and semantic aspects of language; more thorough and methodologically sounder research on parent-child relations as antecedents of later personality development and social behavior; increased concern with positive social behavior (prosocial behavior)—competence, independence, altruism, and moral values. The important theories of developmental psychology are discussed and the significant findings of recent research, as well as established facts, are reviewed.

In discussing each major aspect of development, I have attempted to make clear how the developmental psychologist goes about his work—how he frames research questions, formulates hypotheses, designs his study and selects the research methods to be used, and interprets his findings. Furthermore, the social relevance and the applications of findings to the alleviation of social problems are also stressed.

Like the first edition, this one offers only a *sample* of the major hypotheses, research techniques, and findings of the field, with particular emphasis on *contemporary* directions of theory and research. I hope that the selection of topics and the ideas discussed reflect the broad scope and definition of the field and, at the same time, will stimulate students to think more systematically about problems of human development. This, in turn, may serve to promote a better understanding of the established and potential contributions of this field of research to the advancement of human welfare.

Berkeley, California   PAUL MUSSEN

Introduction

chapter one

Have you ever had an opportunity to observe the development of a young child, even casually? If you have, you were probably fascinated with the rate of his growth and the changes in his behavior. The rapidity of early development is indeed astounding; it hardly seems mystical to speak of "the miracle of growth." The newborn appears tiny and utterly helpless, hardly capable of doing anything—although, as we shall see, he has many capabilities. Yet two years later the baby will be several times as big as he was at birth; he will be walking and beginning to talk. By four, his speech is in many ways like an adult's, his imagination has become much richer, and his thought processes are much more complex than they were just two years earlier.

Can these developments be defined and described precisely? What biological factors and what social experiences produce these striking, rapid changes in the course of development? What processes and mechanisms are involved? These are the fundamental questions of developmental psychology.

Now focus your attention on yourself. What were you like when you were ten years old? Who were your friends and classmates at that time and what were they like? You can probably categorize them into types—

some were bright, ambitious, outgoing, ebullient, "leaders"; some were dull and plodding; some were highly intelligent, shy, studious, not very sociable; a few seemed very independent, out of step with others, apparently unconcerned with what their elders or other children thought, "marching to a different drummer." Of course you could categorize them in many different ways; there were undoubtedly many other "types" of children manifesting other patterns of personality characteristics, interests, abilities, and motives. Obviously, the range of individual differences within any single age group is enormous.

What are the sources of these differences? What are the factors that determine what an individual becomes? What forces shape the individual's abilities, interests, motives, goals, desires, personality characteristics, and social attitudes? To what extent are the differences we observe attributable to "nature"—to genetic or constitutional factors—and to what extent are they the products of "nurture"—environmental factors, early experiences, training, and learning? These questions about the origins of individual differences among children are also basic issues in the field of child psychology.

As a scientific discipline, child psychology is less than a century old, but the problems with which it deals are ancient ones. Many classical philosophers thought and wrote about the characteristics of children and theorized about the determinants of development. Plato, writing in the third century B.C., recognized that individual differences in ability are, to some extent, inborn, but he also realized that early childhood training helps to determine later vocational choice and adjustment. The seventeenth-century English philosopher John Locke believed that strict early discipline was critical for the development of self-discipline and self-control, which in his opinion were cardinal virtues. Jean-Jacques Rousseau, the eighteenth-century French philosopher, agreed with Locke that the experiences of the first few years are crucial in a person's development. He did not, however, believe in early discipline; rather, he advocated permitting children to express their "natural impulses" freely, because he believed these impulses were inherently noble and just.

Other philosophers also speculated and wrote about problems that still concern the child psychologist. But the psychologist does not simply speculate about these problems; he seeks systematic, scientific solutions to them.

The Goals of Child Psychology

Having briefly reviewed some of the fundamental questions of the field, we can turn our attention to the goals and objectives of modern scientific child psychology. The first aim, simply stated, is to describe, as completely and precisely as possible, children's psychological functions (for example, sensory and motor abilities, perception and intellectual functions, social and emotional reactions) at different ages and to discover how these functions change with age.

Data on age trends in development are important for several reasons. The information may be useful in formulating and testing principles of development, that is, generalizations about the sequence or rate of development of psychological functions—perceptual, intellectual, and emotional. Moreover, these data provide averages or norms that can be used in evaluating children's developmental status and in diagnosing problems of physical or psychological development. Is this particular child below or above average in height? Is his intellectual development advanced, retarded, or average for his age? Do his interactions with other children indicate that he is socially mature or immature?

Description of age trends was the predominant goal of child psychology for many years, but recent research in the field has been focused on another goal: the *explanation* of observed age trends. Certainly the phenomena of growth and development must be described before they can be explained. But description itself cannot give us any understanding of why or how developmental changes occur. For instance, the statement that two-year-olds tend to be more negativistic than three-year-olds is merely *descriptive*; it provides no information about the reasons for the two-year-old's negativism. Most child psychologists are concerned with the antecedents of psychological phenomena, including negativism— with the discovery of the processes or mechanisms underlying age changes in growth and behavior. What accounts for the child's becoming less awkward in walking, more fluent in speech, more logical in drawing inferences and solving problems as he grows older?

Another goal, related to the goal of explaining age trends in phenomena, is understanding individual differences and their determinants. If you observe a group of normal four-year-olds in a nursery school, you will find some who talk like adults and some who have meager vocabularies and are infantile in their speech habits and pronunciation. Investigation of such individual differences may contribute to an understanding of the determinants of general age changes in language development. For example, if children who are advanced in speech at this age are found to differ genetically from those who are relatively retarded, you may infer that language facility is, to some extent, dependent on heredity. If, on the other hand, investigation reveals that children advanced in speech receive more encouragement for verbal accomplishment and that they practice speaking more than others, you may infer that improvements with age in language ability are attributable, at least in part, to speech practice and stimulation.

Explanations of age changes and of individual differences—of the hows and whys of development—are enormously complex and draw on findings from several disciplines and several areas of psychology: learning, perception, motivation, social psychology, personality, genetics, physiology, anthropology, sociology, pediatrics. For example, certain physical characteristics (such as height and rate of growth), intelligence, and certain forms of mental deficiency and mental illness are at least in part hereditarily determined. To understand these fully, the developmental psychologist must know something about genetics. The striking physical and behavioral changes of adolescence are strongly influenced by physiological processes involving the endocrine glands and the biochemistry of the blood system; in investigating these phenomena, the psychologist must draw upon findings in physiology and endocrinology. Research in pediatrics has produced pertinent information on the effects of illnesses, malnutrition, and drugs on physical and psychological growth and change. Psychiatry has contributed many facts and theories about how early childhood events affect the behavior and adjustment (or maladjustment) of older children, adolescents, and adults. Many of a person's motives, feelings, attitudes, and interests are strongly conditioned by the social groups to which he belongs, that is, by his social class or by his ethnic or religious-group membership; anthropology and sociology have provided extremely valuable data about the impacts of these elements of social structure on personality, social characteristics, and development. Clearly, a comprehensive understanding of developmental psychology, of age changes and the mechanisms or processes underlying them, involves the integration of many kinds of data drawn from many disciplines.

Explanations of age changes in psychological functions are further complicated by the fact that various aspects of development are closely and intricately interrelated; developments in one function are likely to affect developments in another. For example, while a child is maturing physically (probably, in large measure, as a result of genetic factors), his intelligence is increasing and his abilities to reason and to think logically are improving. At the same time, the child's personality and social behavior are becoming modified partly as a result of these physical and cognitive developments and partly as a result of his own social experiences. In turn, changes in personality and social behavior feed back on, and affect, intelligence and cognitive abilities. In brief, aspects of development interact with and influence one another.

For purposes of discussion, it is often necessary to isolate specific aspects of development such as physical growth, intellectual development, or social behavior, and focus on them separately. This gives a somewhat inaccurate picture of the developmental process. Therefore, the reader must constantly remind himself of the interrelatedness of *all* aspects of development.

In spite of the complexities and intricacies involved in understanding and explaining psychological growth and change, progress in the field of child psychology has been rapid and often exciting, particularly in the last thirty years. We have learned a great deal about children's physical growth, sensory capacities, and perceptual and cognitive abilities (including intelligence), as well as about age changes in these functions. Piaget, the brilliant Swiss psychologist, has given us superb accounts of the stages of development in cognitive functioning, beginning with the newborn's reflex activities and progressing to the adolescent's mature ability to solve problems and to reason. But we do not yet fully understand the processes that account for the transitions from one stage to the next, and there are many other areas in which our knowledge is limited. For example, while there are a number of plausible hypotheses about the effects of early environmental stimulation on later cognitive functioning, scientific evidence is still incomplete. Since this is a significant problem, both theoretically and practically, research in this area has increased substantially in recent years. Many studies show that children from poverty and ghetto areas are deficient in cognitive skills when they enter school. Better understanding of the effects of early stimulation may be practically useful in formulating programs to help prevent, or overcome, these cognitive deficiencies (see pp. 44–46).

A closely related issue is *compensatory education*, an area that has also been the focus of considerable developmental research. Specifically, the questions being asked are: Can preschool training compensate for, or eliminate, some of the cognitive deficiencies that are manifested by ghetto children in school? If so, what kinds of training programs are most effective? Can cognitive development be facilitated or speeded up by training, and if so, under what conditions?

The period of infancy has become a very prominent subject of research in the last few years. Many investigators have found that newborns are much more capable individuals than we had previously suspected; a great many abilities seem to be "wired" or "programmed" into the organism—that is, biologically given, rather than learned. Significant research in the area of language development, part of the field of psycholinguistics, strongly suggests similar conclusions. The acquisition of language cannot be explained on the basis of learning alone; rather, the human nervous system appears to be programmed in ways that make language acquisition possible.

Personality development and social behavior have been, and continue to be, significant research areas. In the past, most research was centered on behaviors such as aggression, dependency, and competition. Many developmental psychologists are still concerned with these topics, but, as we shall see, there has been a marked increase in research on more "positive" social behavior, behavior related to competence, independence, altruism, and moral values.

This volume will review some of the most exciting recent research in child psychology, as well as significant, well-established findings from earlier investigations. We offer a well-selected *sample* of the major ideas, research techniques, and findings of the field. But a brief volume cannot present a complete coverage or survey of the content of the field. Instead our aim is to present an accurate and well-balanced picture of what child psychologists do, how they conduct research, the facts they have discovered, and the social relevance of their research findings.

Research Methods in Child Psychology

To understand, evaluate, and interpret research in child psychology— the *content* of the field—requires knowing something about how the scientist plans his investigations, collects his data, and analyzes his findings. Let us turn our attention briefly to the matter of methods and techniques of research.

The fundamental broad, general method is *unbiased observation.* Observations may be made in *naturalistic* or "real life" settings such as the home, nursery school, playground, park, or the waiting room of a doctor's office. For example, an investigator studying the development of cooperation in children of nursery school age might work with a sample of twenty children. Using the method of time sampling, he would observe each of his subjects extensively for several short periods (perhaps five minutes on each of four different occasions) as they interact with others in the classroom or on the playground. He would record all instances of cooperation between children, such as planning projects together, solving problems jointly, helping each other with tasks, offering suggestions to others, and sharing.

Other observations are made under standardized, controlled conditions, that is, conditions that the investigator sets up. Observations made under these conditions may be more precise and objective than naturalistic observations. If you were investigating the development of children's relationships with children their own age, comparing the earliest reactions with those of older children, you might choose as subjects forty-eight young children—twelve (six boys and six girls) at each of four ages: thirty weeks, forty weeks, fifty weeks, and seventy weeks. You could then bring the children in groups of three into a cheerful, attractively furnished room that had attractive toys and colorful posters, and observe for thirty minutes how the children reacted to each other. The whole episode could be filmed or videotaped and then analyzed very carefully. Frequency and amount of such reactions as smiling, approaching, gesturing, playing together, competing, and fighting would be noted. Comparison of the behaviors of children of different ages would enable you to make some inferences about age trends in early social interactions.

Whenever possible, the investigator uses the most preferred method of scientific research, the experiment, to discover the reasons for changes in behavior. An experiment is another method of controlled observation, but it is distinctive, for it always involves a controlled, prearranged *intervention* or *manipulation* by the experimenter. More specifically, the experimenter actually creates, controls, and varies, *one* particular factor —called the *independent variable*—and then observes whether and how some other variable (or variables), the *dependent* one(s), changes as the independent one is changed. Only one factor is allowed to vary at a time; all others are held constant, that is, not allowed to vary.

To illustrate, suppose we hypothesize that children with phobias about dogs (unusual, intense fear of them) will become less fearful if they observe other children playing happily with dogs and petting them. We could test this hypothesis experimentally by working with two groups of children with dog phobias—and it is not difficult to find a substantial number of such children. Children would be assigned at random to either an experimental group which will observe other children playing with dogs or the control group which will not receive this "treatment." This would be done by putting each child's name on a slip of paper, putting the slips into a hat, mixing them up, and then drawing blindly an equal number for each group. Then we can be sure that the two groups are essentially equal in all respects at the beginning of the experiment; the groups do not differ in any characteristics that might affect response to the "treatment"—age, grade placement, sex, health, intelligence, socio-economic class. We can then control the one variable with which we are concerned, observation of other children playing with dogs.

The children in the experimental group are then brought together for a series of four "parties" at which they are shown movies of a child playing with a dog. As the series progresses, the child in the movie becomes bolder, more vigorous, and more intimate in his approaches to the dog. The control group also has a series of four "parties" during which they see a series of movies, but these movies do not show children playing with animals. Following the series of parties, we could observe each child in a standard situation, bringing him into a large room where there is a dog and carefully noting all of the child's responses. If our original hypothesis is valid, the children in the experimental group will approach the dog without fear and interact with him in play. The control children, on the other hand, will still have their fears, so they will not attempt to approach the dog but will probably avoid him as much as possible. An experiment very much like this has actually been conducted with impressive findings that support the hypothesis (see pp. 88–89).

The most critical feature of the experimental procedure is that it permits precise and accurate evaluations of the effects of experimental treatments. Thus, in our example, we could measure precisely how watching films of fearless children affected children's fears of dogs. Without a controlled experiment, it would be impossible to assess the relative contributions of each of the many variables that affect the development and reduction of fear—factors such as sex, social class, presence or absence of supportive adults, rewards or punishments for showing or inhibiting fear responses. Clinical and observational studies of fear reduction might yield valuable information about the influences of some of these variables, but these variables can be isolated and their effects precisely assessed only by experimental means.

Unfortunately, there are many important problems in child psychology that simply cannot be investigated experimentally. For example, it is important to determine precisely the effects of parental rejection on the child's personality development, but we can hardly expect parents to reject their children just so someone can conduct an experiment. Obviously, other methods must be used to study problems like this.

Parents can be interviewed regarding their child-rearing practices, the nature and extent of their interactions with the child, their expression of affection toward him, methods of punishment, the amount of time spent doing things together. The interview data can then be analyzed and parental rejection (or permissiveness, or punitiveness, or warmth) can be *rated*. These ratings of parental practices can then be correlated with measures of children's personality, derived from observations or tests. Unfortunately, however, the interview technique has many shortcomings; parents may not be good observers of their own behavior, their memories may be selective, or their reports may be biased.

Parent-child relationships may be assessed by means of another naturalistic method, the *home visit*. The home visitor, a trained observer, goes to the child's home and observes families in their normal interactions for a few hours on several occasions. These careful observations are the bases for evaluating variables such as parental warmth, rejection, permissiveness, or control. If, however, the presence of the home visitor inhibits the behavior of the members of the family—if their interactions are not natural or spontaneous when the visitor is there—the behavior sample will hardly give an accurate picture of family relationships.

A relatively new, quasi-naturalistic method, *structured observation*, is proving to be very fruitful in investigations of parent-child relationships. A parent and child are brought together in a standard situation that evokes interaction. For example, they might be presented with complicated play equipment and told that they can use it in any way they want. The situation elicits a sample of habitual, natural interactions and thus gives the investigator an opportunity to observe and rate such variables as a mother's (or father's) ability to motivate her child, reaction to child's needs and interests, use of praise or punishment, supportiveness, control, methods of enforcing rules, and permissiveness.

LONGITUDINAL AND CROSS-SECTIONAL APPROACHES

The two basic approaches to the study of human development are the *longitudinal* and the *cross-sectional*. These can best be explained as contrasting methods. In the longitudinal approach, the same group of children is studied, tested, and observed repeatedly over an extended period of time. For example, in investigating the development of reasoning ability and concept formation between the ages of four and ten longitudinally, a researcher would gather a group of subjects and give them appropriate tests, first when they were four years old, and subsequently at annual or semiannual intervals until they were ten. Analysis of the results of his tests would permit him to define age trends in the development of these functions.

An investigator employing the cross-sectional method to study these developments would give these tests all at once to children of different ages, that is, to samples of four-year-olds, five-year-olds, six-year-olds, and so forth. Comparison of the performances of children of different ages would, as in the case of the longitudinal study, enable him to describe age trends in problem-solving and concept-formation ability.

There are several kinds of problems that can be adequately investigated only by means of the longitudinal method, however. For example, the study of *individual* trends in development must be longitudinal, for it requires repeated testing. We can determine whether personality, intelligence, or performance are stable, or consistent, over long periods of time only if we test the same individuals at different ages—a longitudinal approach. And we can most adequately evaluate latent or delayed effects of early experiences, such as parental overprotection, in later personality by longitudinal means—that is, by relating observations of early treatment to personality data collected later in the child's life.

Although it is very useful, the longitudinal method is extremely expensive and time-consuming, and it has some inherent limitations. For instance, we know little or nothing of how repeated exposure to psychological testing and observation affects the subjects in such studies, or of the possible biases investigators might develop as a result of their frequent contacts with the subjects. For these reasons, the method has been used only in a limited number of studies; the cross-sectional method has been used much more frequently in child psychology.

ETHICAL CONSIDERATIONS IN RESEARCH

Most psychologists hope that their scientific work will prove to be useful in promoting human welfare. Findings from research in child psychology may be used in helping people to achieve better adjustment and happier lives; in overcoming early-established cognitive deficiencies; in facilitating effective learning and greater creativity; in reducing prejudices, fears, and anxieties; in fostering altruistic, cooperative, humanitarian attitudes and behaviors.

In order to achieve such goals, the psychologist must study people—and the use of human subjects involves many ethical responsibilities. A paramount duty of the investigator is guarding the welfare of his subjects and respecting their rights. Experiments on the effects of cruelty, neglect, or extreme deprivation during infancy on later behavior and maladjustment might have great potential practical benefits, but no ethical psychologist would subject infants to such treatments.

Unfortunately, the ethical issues in most research are much less obvious. Is it ethical to subject children to frustration or stress—even of a mild sort—for experimental purposes? Should parents be asked to reveal information that might embarrass them? Should an investigator attempt to accelerate learning or improve the cognitive skills of children from disadvantaged families, risking the possibility that the experimental subjects may become more dissatisfied with their life situations or have great conflicts with their families? Of course, there are no satisfactory, pat answers to these questions, no formulas that investigators can apply in solving their ethical problems. However, some general principles and guidelines have been formulated and written into "ethical codes" by committees of the American Psychological Association. Here, in abbreviated form, are some of these principles.

The investigator must take all possible steps to guarantee the privacy of his subjects and is ethically bound to protect any confidential information he receives. Participation in a study must be voluntary—although in the case of young children the parents may have to do the volunteering —and subjects should be informed of the nature of the investigation, including any possible stress or discomfort. The investigator has an obligation to insure that no permanent physical or psychological harm will result from the research procedures, and he must make all possible efforts to relieve any temporary discomfort or stress that the subjects suffer. In addition, he should give the subjects some understanding of their role in the collection of data and of the potential benefit of the study to others.

Obviously, guidelines such as these are broad and general; they cannot cover all possible ethical dilemmas. Codes cannot be a substitute for honesty, integrity, sensitivity, and goodwill on the part of investigators. They alone are responsible for making mature ethical judgments about the conduct of their research and for applying the highest moral principles in making their decisions.

General Principles of Development and Development in Infancy

Development is a continuous process that begins when life does, at conception—at the moment the mother's egg (ovum) is fertilized, its wall being penetrated by a sperm cell from the father. Immediately following conception, the process of *mitosis*, or cell division, is initiated. The fertilized ovum, a single cell, divides and subdivides rapidly, until millions of cells have been formed. As development proceeds, the new cells assume highly specialized functions, becoming parts of various body systems—nervous, skeletal, muscular, or circulatory. The fetus, as a child is called before it is born, begins to take shape.

The sequence of development in the prenatal (before-birth) period is fixed and invariable. The head, eyes, trunk, arms, legs, genitals, and internal organs develop in the same order and at approximately the same prenatal ages in all fetuses. Just about nine months after conception, the child is born.

While the processes underlying growth are extremely complex, both before and after birth, human development proceeds in accordance with a number of general principles. The most important ones are summarized in the following paragraphs.

1. Growth and changes in behavior are orderly and, for the most part,

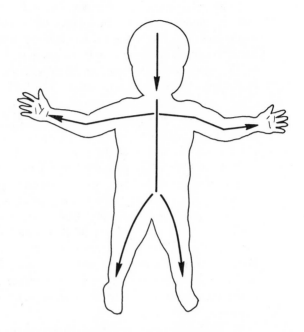

FIGURE 2.1   Diagrammatic representation of directions of growth.

occur in unvarying sequences. All fetuses can turn their heads before
they can extend their hands. After birth, there are definite patterns of
physical growth and of increases in motor and cognitive abilities. Every
child sits before he stands, stands before he walks, draws a circle before
he draws a square. All babies go through the same sequence of stages in
speech development, babbling before talking, pronouncing certain sounds
before others. Certain cognitive abilities invariably precede others; all
children can categorize objects or put them into a series according to
size before they can think logically or formulate hypotheses.

The patterned nature of early physical and motor development is
neatly illustrated in "directional" trends. One is the *cephalocaudal* or
head-to-foot direction of development of form and function. For example, the fetus's arm buds (the beginnings of his arms) appear before
leg buds and his head is well developed before his legs are well formed.
In the infant, visual fixation and eye-hand coordination are perfected
long before the arms and hands can be used effectively in reaching and
grasping. Following the *proximodistal* or *outward* direction of development, the central parts of the body mature earlier and become functional
before those toward the periphery. Efficient movements of the arm and
forearm precede those of the wrist, hands, and fingers. The upper arm

and upper leg are brought under voluntary control before the forearm, foreleg, hands, and feet. The infant's earliest acts are gross, diffuse, and undifferentiated, involving the whole body or large segments of it. Gradually, however, these are replaced by more refined, differentiated, and precise actions—a developmental trend from *mass to specific activity*, from large- to small-muscle action. The baby's initial attempts to grasp a cube are very clumsy compared with the refined thumb-and-forefinger movements he can make a few months later; his first steps in walking are awkward and involve excessive movements, but gradually he walks more gracefully and precisely.

2. Development is patterned and continuous, but it is not always smooth and gradual. There are periods of very rapid physical growth—growth spurts—and of extraordinary increments in psychological abilities. For example, the baby's height and weight increase enormously during the first year, and preadolescents and adolescents grow unusually rapidly as well. The genital organs develop very slowly during childhood but very rapidly during adolescence. During the preschool period, there are sharp increases in vocabulary and motor skills, and around adolescence the individual's ability to solve logical problems undergoes remarkable improvement.

3. There are critical or sensitive periods in the development of certain body organs and psychological functions. Interference with normal development at these periods may result in permanent deficiencies or malfunctions. For example, there are critical periods in the development of the fetus's heart, eyes, lungs, and kidneys; if the course of normal development is interrupted at one of these periods—perhaps as a result of maternal virus infection or German measles (rubella)—the child may suffer permanent organ damage.

Erik Erikson, a prominent child psychoanalyst and theorist, considers the first year of life to be a critical period for the development of trust in others. The infant who does not experience adequate warmth, love, and gratification of needs during this time may fail to develop a sense of trust, and consequently may fail to form satisfactory relationships at later times. Analogously, there seem to be periods of "readiness" for learning various tasks, such as reading or bicycle riding. The child who does not learn these tasks during these periods may have great difficulty learning them later.

4. The child's experiences at one stage of development affect his later development. If a pregnant woman suffers severe malnourishment, the child she is carrying may not develop the normal number of brain cells and may therefore be born mentally defective. Infants who spend their first months in very dull, unstimulating environments appear to be deficient in cognitive skills and perform poorly on tests of intellectual

function in later childhood. The child who receives too little warmth, love, and attention in the first year fails to develop self-confidence and trust early in life and is likely to become an emotionally unstable and maladjusted child at adolescence.

5. All the individual's characteristics and abilities, as well as all developmental changes, are the products of two basic, though complex, processes: *maturation* (organic, neurophysiological-biochemical changes occurring within an individual's body that are relatively independent of external environmental conditions, experiences, or practice) and *experience* (learning and practice).

Since learning and maturation almost always interact, it is difficult to

FIGURE 2.2. The development of posture and locomotion in infants. (From Shirley, M. M. *The first two years, a study of twenty-five babies: Vol. II, Intellectual Development. Inst. Child Welfare Monogr.* Ser. No. 8. Minneapolis: University of Minnesota Press, 1933. With permission of the University of Minnesota Press.)

separate their effects or to specify their relative contributions to psychological development. Certainly, prenatal growth and changes in body proportions and in the structure of the nervous system are products of maturational processes rather than of experiences. In contrast, the development of motor skills and cognitive functions depend on *both* maturation and experience, and on the interaction between the two. In large measure, maturational forces determine *when* the child is ready to walk; restrictions on practice do not ordinarily postpone the onset of walking—unless the restrictions are extreme. Many Hopi Indian infants are kept bound to cradle-boards most of the time for the first three months of their lives and for part of each day after that. Therefore, they have very little experience using the muscles used in walking; yet they begin to walk at the same age as other children. Conversely, you cannot teach a baby to stand or walk until his neural and muscular apparatus have matured sufficiently. Once these basic motor skills are acquired, however, they improve with experience and practice. Walking becomes better coordinated and more graceful as waste movements are eliminated; steps become longer, straighter, and more rapid.

Language acquisition and the development of cognitive skills are also outcomes of the interaction between experiential and maturational forces. Babies do not begin to talk or to put words together until they attain a certain level of maturity, regardless of how much "teaching" they are given. But obviously the language the child acquires depends on his experiences—the language he hears others speaking—and his verbal facility will be at least partly a function of the encouragement and rewards he gets for verbal expression.

Analogously, the child will not acquire certain cognitive or intellectual skills until he has reached a certain stage of maturity. For example, until what Piaget calls the operational stage—roughly ages six or seven—the child deals only with objects and events and representations of these; he does not really deal with ideas or concepts. Before he reaches the operational stage he has not attained the concept of *conservation*—the idea that the quantity of a substance, such as clay, does not change simply because its shape is changed, for example, from a ball to a hot dog. However, once he has reached the stage of concrete operations and has more experience with the notion of conservation, he can apply it to other qualities; that is, he understands that length, mass, number, and weight remain constant in spite of certain changes in external appearance.

6. Almost all human characteristics are the products of a series of complex interactions between *heredity (genetic factors)* and *environment (experience)*. It is extremely difficult to disentangle the effects of two sets of determinants on observed characteristics; the general question of heredity *or* environment is often essentially meaningless. Consider, for example, the case of the son of a successful businessman and his school-

teacher wife. The boy's IQ is 140, which is very high. Is this the product of his inheritance of high potential or of a stimulating home environment? Most likely it is the outcome of the *interaction* between these.

We can, of course, consider genetic influences on specific characteristics, such as height, intelligence, or aggressiveness. But, in most instances of psychological functions, the exact contributions of hereditary factors are unknown. For such characteristics, the relevant questions are: Which of the individual's genetic potentialities will be actualized in the physical, social, and cultural environment in which he develops? What limits to development of psychological functions are set by the individual's genetic constitution?

Many aspects of physique and appearance are strongly influenced by genetic factors—sex, eye and skin color, shape of the face, height, and weight. But environmental factors may even exert strong influences on some of these characteristics that are primarily genetically determined. For example, the American-born children of Jewish immigrants two generations ago grew taller and weighed more than their parents and their brothers and sisters born abroad. Children of the present generation in the United States and other Western countries are taller and heavier, and grow more rapidly, than children of earlier generations. Clearly, then, environmental factors, especially nutrition and living conditions, affect physique and rate of growth.

Genetic factors influence temperamental characteristics such as tendencies to be calm and relaxed or high-strung and quick to react. Heredity may also set limits beyond which intelligence cannot develop. But how and under what conditions temperamental characteristics or intelligence will be manifested depends on many environmental factors. A child with good intellectual potential, genetically determined, will not be highly intelligent if he is reared in a dull, unstimulating environment or if he has no motivation to use his potential. We shall discuss this matter further (see pp. 43–46).

In brief, relative contributions of hereditary and environmental forces vary from characteristic to characteristic. In asking about possible genetic influences on behavior, we must always be concerned with the conditions under which the characteristics are manifested. In the case of most behavioral characteristics, the contributions of hereditary factors are unknown and indirect.

THE STUDY OF INFANTS

For both theoretical and practical reasons, the study of infancy has become increasingly important since the early 1960s. Several of the broad general principles of development discussed above were derived from research with infants. Most importantly, human development depends to a great extent on learning and experience, and in order to understand these processes we must know the bases on which learning must be built, that is, the needs, sensory capacities, and response capabilities the individual starts with.

Of course, there are basic, innate biological needs—needs for oxygen, for food and drink, for elimination, for temperature regulation. The ancients were aware of the fact that neonates (newborns) have many motor reflexes (automatic, involuntary responses) that have survival value. These include *sucking* to get milk and *pupillary reflexes* (contraction of the pupils of the eyes as protection against bright lights or flashes).

Some new and exciting research demonstrates that the newborn is a remarkably capable organism and has much more cognitive ability than had been realized in the past. Almost from the moment of birth, the infant is able to learn and some rather complex perceptual capacities, and some kinds of understanding previously believed to be products of learning and experience now appear to be "programmed" into the organism. Before turning to these fascinating new findings, let us briefly survey the neonate's physical characteristics, needs, and sensory capacities.

Characteristics of Neonates

PHYSICAL GROWTH

The infant's body grows extremely rapidly during the first year, when relative increases in length and weight are greater than at any later time. The baby's birth weight—about seven pounds on the average for boys and slightly less for girls—doubles during the first six months and almost triples in the first year. Body length, for boys about twenty inches at birth on the average, increases over one-third, to about twenty-eight or twenty-nine inches by the end of the first year.

During infancy, different parts of the body grow at different rates until body proportions become more like an adult's. In accordance with the head-to-foot principle of development, the head and upper parts of the body grow at a faster pace than the trunk and legs. Head size increases at an amazing rate, beginning almost immediately after conception, and by birth the head is about 60 percent as large as it will be in adulthood. A newborn baby appears to be top-heavy, the length of his head being one-quarter of his total body length. Brain size doubles during the first two years. The trunk ranks second to the head in overall growth rate, reaching approximately half of its full (adult) length by the end of the second year. Of all the parts of the neonate's body, his legs are furthest from adult size, and relative to the upper parts of the body they grow slowly.

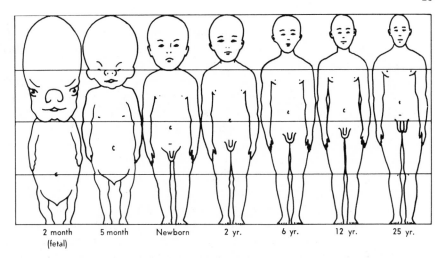

2 month (fetal)	5 month	Newborn	2 yr.	6 yr.	12 yr.	25 yr.

FIGURE 2.3. Changes in form and proportion of the human body during fetal and postnatal life. (From C. M. Jackson. Some aspects of form and growth, in W. J. Robbins, S. Brody, A. F. Hogan, C. M. Jackson, and C. W. Green (eds.), *Growth*. New Haven: Yale University Press, 1929, p. 118. By permission.)

NEONATAL NEEDS

Many of the infant's innate biological needs are gratified in self-regulatory ways, that is, without voluntary control or active participation by the infant or by others. For example, reflex breathing mechanisms provide enough oxygen to take care of the neonate's requirements. The reflexive sphincter takes care of his need for elimination, and under ordinary circumstances automatic physiological reactions keep his body at a relatively constant temperature. The body's chemical and physiological balances, and thus energy, are maintained through sleep; unless the infant is ill, in pain, or extremely hungry or uncomfortable, he will sleep as much as he needs to and awaken when he is rested.

Two prominent biological needs, hunger and thirst, are not satisfied automatically. If no one helps the infant to gratify these needs promptly, tensions may become intense and painful. The social relationships related to satisfaction of these needs are among the infant's most important early experiences and may have enduring effects on his later development (see pp. 60–63).

SENSORY AND PERCEPTUAL ABILITIES

The infant's sensory system is remarkably well developed at birth. He can see, hear, and smell, and he is sensitive to pain, touch, and change of position. While his sense of taste is not well developed at first, he reacts to differences in sweet-tasting and sour-tasting substances within the first two weeks. Sensitivity to pain, already present at birth, becomes keener within the first few days. Coordination and convergence of the eyes, required for visual fixation and for depth perception, begin to develop immediately after birth and appear to be fairly well established by the age of seven or eight weeks. Infants as young as fifteen days of age can discriminate differences in brightness and hue. Swing a bright object before the infant or project a moving colored spot on the ceiling above, and he will follow it with his eyes.

Since the newborn's sensory organs function well, he is sensitive to many stimuli. But he does not attend to everything equally; he focuses his attention much more on some stimuli than on others. Stimuli with a "high rate of change"—those that move, or have marked contrasts between light and dark, or have a great deal of contour (black edge on white background)—are likely to attract and hold the newborn's attention. When his eyes are open, he searches until he finds some contour edges and then he focuses on these edges. Because he searches actively and attends differentially to various stimuli, the newborn appears to be absorbing and storing information, yet it seems unlikely that he *perceives* the world as adults do. Perception involves the organization and interpretation of simple sense impressions, and mature perception by and large requires neurological development, experience, and learning.

It now appears that a number of rather complex perceptual abilities traditionally thought to be products of learning are probably innate. Take, for example, the perception of solidity; earlier writings suggested that the ability to identify objects as solid is the result of learning to associate visual cues with tactile impressions. Some ingenious recent research suggests that this is not the case, however. By placing polarizing goggles over an infant's eyes and using polarizing filters and rear-projection screens, the experimenter created an optical illusion—a cube appearing in front of a screen looking very real and solid. It was, however, intangible; when the infant attempted to grasp it he felt only empty air. Every one of the infant subjects in the experiment, ranging in age from twelve to twenty-four weeks, showed marked surprise (crying and startled responses) when he reached for the cube and felt nothing. The younger infants simply cried and their facial expressions changed; the older ones reacted more strongly, staring at their hands and appearing very startled. None of these infants showed any signs of surprise when they felt real objects suspended before them. The investigator interpreted the infants' surprise when they reached for the illusory object as evidence that they "expected" an object to be solid and touchable. If this expectation depends on learning to coordinate vision and touch, this learning must take place before the age of twelve weeks.

To rule out the possibility that the infants' surprise was due to very early learning, the investigator began to work with even younger infants, two-week-olds. At this age, babies ordinarily show a defensive response when a solid object approaches them. They pull their heads back or put their hands between their face and the object, as though to shield themselves. These responses are accompanied by distress and crying—often very vigorous crying. Again using projectors and goggles, the investigator moved an illusory object toward the neonate's face. All the infants tested exhibited defensive reactions. The investigator therefore concluded that there is a built-in association between visual objects and the expectation that they are solid and can be touched.

Consider another complex kind of perception, the perception of depth. Many species of animals are born with the ability to perceive depth— and thus to avoid falling into crevices—and depth perception is apparently acquired very early in humans. In one experiment, babies a few months of age were placed, individually, in the center of a heavy solid glass rectangle. Extending from the center on one side was a checkerboard pattern, placed directly beneath the glass. On the other side, the same kind of pattern was placed several feet below the glass, thus giving the illusion of depth or a visual cliff. If the infant's mother came to the "shallow" end of the table and called to him, he would readily crawl to her. If she called to him from the "deep" side, however, he would not cross the cliff or approach her, *even though he could pat the glass and knew that the surface was solid.* This suggests that the ability to perceive depth is innate.

While attention to movement and to contrast are clearly unlearned responses, experience very soon begins to play a role in attention. If you show one- or two-week-old newborns a black and white outline of a human face and a meaningless design, they will look equally long at each of them, for both stimuli contain strong contrasts. However, four-month-old infants show much longer fixations (greater attention) to outlines of faces than they do to meaningless designs. By this age, the infant's attention has become more selective; he is attracted more to familiar and meaningful stimuli than to meaningless ones.

LEARNING IN NEONATES AND INFANTS

Infants are capable of learning from the very first few days of life. A newborn can be conditioned to turn his head to one side in response to the sound of a bell coming from that direction. During conditioning trials in one experiment, each time a bell was sounded to the left side of the newborn's head and he responded by turning his head in that direction, he received a nipple to suck on and milk. If he did not turn his head during the first few trials, the nipple was brushed against the lower left corner of his mouth lightly to elicit head turning, a reflex response to this stimulation.

In each experimental session, the sound of a bell was paired with the nipple ten times. During the first sessions, the infant sometimes turned his head to the left when the bell sounded and sometimes he did not. After seventeen or eighteen such experimental sessions—a total of about 175 trials—infants as young as three days learned to turn their heads toward the nipple every time they heard the bell. Of course this kind of conditioning can be achieved much more rapidly in older infants. Thus, three-month-old babies become conditioned in about one-quarter of the number of trials (about 40) that it takes to condition a three-day-old.

Very early in life, experience and reward begin to affect the frequency with which infants manifest "social responses" such as cooing and smiling. Three-month-old babies in one experiment were rewarded by an experimenter every time they made sounds. The rewards were being smiled at or touched lightly on the abdomen. Following these rewards, the frequency of the infants' vocalizations increased greatly, compared to what it had been before the experiment began. When the experimenter stopped rewarding the vocalizations, their frequency decreased to a baseline level. In another study, an infant was rewarded (picked up, smiled at, and talked to) every time he smiled. After this, he smiled much more frequently, but when rewards were discontinued, the frequency of smiles diminished significantly, and protests (crying, kicking, and howling) increased. These experiments demonstrate that even very young infants learn responses that lead to rewards; through rewards, adults can exert a significant degree of control over an infant's behavior.

Nevertheless, many prominent psychological theorists maintain that the infant *actively participates in learning*—that his behavior is *not* controlled, shaped, and molded primarily by external forces and rewards, but rather that the infant *intends* to learn and *initiates* learning. Pertinent evidence for this point of view comes from the experimental work of Professor Jerome Bruner and his colleagues at the Center for Cognitive Studies at Harvard University. These researchers showed that infants could learn to "regulate" or "control" a reflex response such as sucking in order to produce satisfying changes in their environment. Each of their subjects—infants four, five, or six weeks of age—was seated in a high chair in front of a panel of colored lightbulbs. In the infant's mouth was placed a pacifier nipple connected to an electrical system so that if the infant sucked in long, hard bursts colored bulbs flashed on and off, giving a "light show." Infants learned immediately, during the very first experimental session, to suck in ways that produced this desirable show. If conditions were reversed so that hard sucking turned off the lights, they quickly learned to desist from sucking this way. The infants' learning was so rapid that it cannot be explained simply as the result of rewards. Rather, the investigators conclude that there is some kind of inherent predisposition—a kind of built-in program of action in the infant's mind—that permits babies to pick up rules quickly and to establish cause-and-effect relationships between what they do and what they perceive. They believe that conditioning requires a great deal of time because infants are adverse to such learning; when the infant uses his own initiative, fulfills his own intentions, and is active in the process, he learns very quickly.

This emphasis on the infant's active role in learning is also characteristic of the theories of Jean Piaget, the most influential developmental psychologist of this century. Piaget is an acute observer of children and he uses both naturalistic observation and informal experimental techniques in his research. The subjects of his earliest observations were his own children, but he subsequently expanded the population he observed tremendously.

For Piaget, intelligence is the ability to adapt to the environment and to new situations—to think and act in adaptive ways. Furthermore, in his view children always play an active and creative part in their own cognitive development. As we shall see later (see pp. 31–36), cognitive development proceeds in a regular, invariant sequence of stages; that is, every child goes through the same succession of stages of development. The sequence is neither biologically determined nor the direct result of experience. Instead, cognitive development is the outcome of a continuous interaction between the *structure* of the organism and the environment. At each stage, the child has certain mental capabilities and certain organizing tendencies, and these influence the ways in which the child interacts with or "operates on" the environment and his experiences. Experience is a necessary element in cognitive development, but experience does not direct or shape development; the child actively selects, orders, organizes, and interprets his experiences.

According to Piaget's theory, the first stage of cognitive development, the one with which we are concerned here, is the *sensorimotor period*, extending from birth to about eighteen months or two years of age. During this time, the child's perceptions improve and he performs increasingly complex actions; but he does not have mental representation or thought processes that depend on symbolic language. The infant's intelligence progresses from simple reflexes and vague awareness of the environment to more distinct, complex, and precise perceptions and increasingly more systematic and well-organized responses.

The *sensorimotor* period is divided into six phases. For the first month, the infant actively exercises the reflexes present at birth (his only mental "structures" at this time); as a result these become modified, elaborated, and more efficient. The second phase, which lasts from roughly one to four months, involves *coordination of reflexes and responses.* Hand movements become coordinated with eye movements; what he hears he looks at (orienting reflex); he reaches for objects, grasps and sucks them. If by chance one of his actions produces an enjoyable result, he immediately attempts to repeat this action. For example, if he finds that sucking his hand is enjoyable, he begins to make active efforts to insert his hand into his mouth.

In the third phase, approximately four to eight months, the infant begins to crawl and to manipulate objects. He shows interest in the environment and he begins to anticipate the consequences of his actions, *intentionally* repeating actions that produce interesting and enjoyable results. For example, at four months of age a baby will kick his legs in order to make a toy suspended over his crib swing. Moreover, since he is now interested in the objective world, he begins to look for objects he has lost sight of.

In the fourth phase, the child begins to differentiate means from ends, and he uses previously learned responses to attain goals. Thus, if a desirable toy is hidden from his view, he will actively search for it and he will remove an obstacle in order to get it.

The fifth phase, beginning at eleven or twelve months of age, is characterized by active experimentation, novelty-seeking exploration, variation, and modification of behavior. The child appears to be genuinely interested in novelty and manifests a great deal of curiosity. He experiments a great deal, dropping objects just to watch them fall, pulling toys toward him with strings, and using sticks to push things around. His activities become more deliberate, constructive, and original.

Between eighteen months and two years of age the child is in the sixth and final phase of the sensorimotor period, one that represents a very important cognitive advance. In this phase we see the real beginnings of the capacity to respond to or think about objects and events that are not immediately observable. The child begins to *invent* new means of accomplishing goals through "mental combinations," that is, through imagination and ideas. He "thinks out" a problem before he attempts to solve it, and he uses ideas and images to invent new ways of accomplishing goals. Objects may be considered in new relationships to one another. Thus, the child may use a stick as a tool for drawing an object toward him even though he has never used a stick in this way previously. Problem solving, remembering, planning, imagining, and pretending are all possible at this stage.

Obviously the infant makes tremendous cognitive progress between birth and 2 years of age. His development is gradual and continuous rather than abrupt and sudden. Starting from an undifferentiated state in which he hardly distinguishes himself from the environment and can react only in reflex ways, he moves to a level of genuine intelligence—to a stage in which he can represent objects mentally, solve problems, and invent new ways of doing things.

Language, Cognitive Development, and Intelligence

For normal children, infancy ends with the beginnings of real language. As we noted, in Piaget's theory the first period of cognitive development, the sensorimotor, is completed when the child begins to use images and symbols, including language, in his thinking. We shall return to Piaget's theory of cognitive development after infancy shortly; before doing that, we shall take a closer look at language acquisition and its influence on cognition.

It would be difficult to overestimate the importance of language in a child's development. A major part of his learning—at home, in the neighborhood, in school, and from the mass media—depends on language, the basis of all social communication. The functioning of the social structure and the transmission of culture from one generation to the next depend largely on language.

Language is also involved in almost all higher mental processes—in almost all cognition—such as thinking, abstraction, concept formation, planning, reasoning, remembering, judging, and solving problems. Therefore, it is hardly surprising that the child's cognitive abilities progress markedly as he acquires language and as his verbal facility improves. After the child acquires some names or labels that are applied to objects or events, such as "dog," or "Grandma coming," he is likely to react in the same way to all stimuli that have these labels (approaching and petting four-legged animals called dogs and smiling when Grandma arrives). This is known as *verbal mediation* or *mediated generalization*, and the importance of such mediation in concept formation, abstraction, problem solving, thinking, and learning has been demonstrated repeatedly.

To illustrate, in transposition experiments subjects learn to make choices on the basis of *relationships* among stimuli. Suppose, for example, a child first learns to choose the largest of three squares. Later, he is presented with three different squares, the smallest of them being the same size as the largest one (the "correct" one) of the previous trials. Young children with limited language ability find it very difficult to learn to respond to the *relative* sizes of the objects. Instead, they choose in terms of the absolute size of the stimulus. Older children who know— and can apply—words (verbal mediators) like "biggest" or "middle-size," learn transposition or relational choices very easily.

Abstraction and concept formation are required for successful *reversal learning*, in which a child must learn to do the opposite of what he has previously done in the same situation. To illustrate, experimental subjects may be taught to discriminate between two stimuli that differ in both size and color. Choice of the larger of two squares, regardless of its color, is rewarded; that is, the attribute of size is the relevant one, while color is irrelevant. Subsequently there is a *reversal shift* in the pattern of rewards in the experiment: the attribute of size is still the relevant one, but this time the child is rewarded for choosing the smaller rather than the larger one. (In the *nonreversal shift* the previously irrelevant attribute becomes pertinent. Whereas rewards previously depended on discriminating on the basis of size, they would now be contingent on choices based on color.)

Children who can make mediating verbal responses—who can say to themselves, "It's the size that's important"—find it relatively easy to learn the reversal shift. Experimental data show that as verbal skills improve, reversal shifts are mastered more easily. Nursery school children find such learning difficult, and only a few of them readily learn to shift. Among kindergarten children, those who are fast learners (presumably bright, verbal children) have little difficulty mastering reversal shifts; slow learners do not learn the shift as easily.

If preschool children are taught to verbalize the relevant dimension (to say "large" when making the discrimination), they can master the reversal shift; but children who learn to verbalize the irrelevant dimension or do not make any mediating response find the task difficult. Among the subjects in a complex experimental study, only 25 per cent of the three-year-olds responded on the basis of reversal shift, but this proportion rose gradually with age; 62 percent of the ten-year-olds, the oldest ones in the study, responded this way. Apparently the ability to learn reversal shifts depends on having a concept (verbal mediation) of the critical dimension, and with greater skill in language it is easier to acquire such concepts.

With better perception, a wider variety of experiences, and increased vocabulary and language ability, the child's concepts become more refined and more sharply differentiated. By the time he is five or six, the child has many concepts pertaining to his physical environment, inanimate objects, home, family, and neighborhood. By and large, these are concrete concepts, attached to real objects and their external characteristics. He is just beginning to acquire concepts of numbers and abstract ideas, which, as we shall see, develop more fully during the early school years.

While language development facilitates complex cognitive functioning, it should not be inferred that it is not possible to think or reason without language. Deaf children are only slightly handicapped in many intellectual and cognitive tasks, including tests of reasoning, even though they are considerably retarded in verbal ability and, in many cases, never acquire adequate verbal skills. In brief, while we often use language in thinking, it is possible to think without using language.

LANGUAGE DEVELOPMENT

Since the late 1950s the field of psycholinguistics—the psychological study of language and its development—has become very prominent and productive. Large samples of children's vocalizations and speech have been recorded and minutely analyzed. And, although the process of language is not fully understood, it has become apparent that children's language has definite, structural properties. Clearly the child's experiences have powerful impacts on his language acquisition; babies learn to speak the language they hear others around them speaking. A child cannot acquire a label or concept of something that is not part of the culture in which he grows up. If wigwams or igloos are unknown in his culture, he cannot form concepts of these things. An American child acquires only one label for rice; an Indonesian child has labels for many types of rice and differentiates among these: rice in the paddies, mature but unharvested rice, boiled rice, and so forth.

Psycholinguists offer impressive arguments that biological, maturational processes also loom large in language development. The development of phonemes, the most elementary speech sounds, follows an unvaried sequence that strongly suggests a maturational basis. Sounds formed at the back of the mouth, such as *h*, ordinarily appear first and decrease in relative frequency as sounds involving the use of the teeth and lips become more common. Children of all nations and cultures make the same sounds and in the same order. English and American infants pronounce French nasals and French gutteral r's as well as German vowel sounds, and deaf babies utter the same phonemes—and at about the same time—as children who hear normally. All babies coo and babble, repeating the same sound over again (for example, "da da da da") from about the third month until the end of the first year, and imitation of adult speech generally begins at about nine months of age. New sounds are not learned by imitation, however; the baby imitates only those sounds that he has already uttered spontaneously.

The most impressive of the psycholinguists' arguments about the overriding importance of maturation concern the amazingly rapid development of the child's comprehension and use of language, particularly his early mastery of grammar. While no real language appears before eighteen months of age, even complex rules of grammar are acquired by about three-and-a-half or four years of age. Hence, the psycholinguists argue that a basis for the rich and intricate competence of adult grammar must emerge in the short span of twenty-four months.

Even casual observation tells us that comprehension of language precedes linguistic performance. The average baby will respond to simple commands at about ten months of age, but will not speak his first word until a few months later. Generally that word is a single or duplicated syllable, such as "dada," and it may function as a whole sentence meaning "Where is Daddy?" or "I see Daddy."

At approximately eighteen months of age children begin putting words together in simple, primitive sentences. Nevertheless, analysis reveals that these sentences have grammatical structure, that is, they follow definite rules of word order. In so-called "pivotal constructions" a small class of *pivot words* always occupies the first or second position in a two-word sentence, and many other *open* words can occur in either position. In the following sentences *see* would be regarded as a pivot word in the first position and *gone* would be a second-position pivot word: "See baby," "See milk," "See hat"; "Milk gone," "Mamma gone," "Walk gone." After a slow start, pivotal constructions develop rapidly during the third year. The number of open words grows more rapidly than the number of pivots. Open words are often used alone, but pivot words do not ordinarily appear in isolation; they are always in a fixed position, first or second, relative to the open words. The child's two-word sentences are not generally simple imitations of others' speech; many of these have not been heard previously. In short, even at this stage the child generates (creates) new sentences.

During the third year, the child's vocabulary increases at a remarkably rapid rate, and longer strings of words are put together in sentences. These too follow grammatical rules, some of them quite complex.

The speech of the four-year-old reveals that he has acquired most of the important grammatical rules governing word order, the formation of plurals, and of past and future tenses. Even his grammatical errors reveal his knowledge of grammar. For example, a four-year-old may say, "We *drawed* pictures of *gooses* in school." Since *drawed* and *gooses* are not correct forms, they are clearly not imitations of adult speech. Yet, in using these words, the child demonstrates that he has acquired the rules for forming past tense and plurals, although he has overgeneralized these rules, treating irregular words as though they were regular ones.

The child's early acquisition of grammar and the amazingly rapid development of his ability to generate new sentences are extremely difficult to explain on the basis of learning and experience. Noam Chomsky, a distinguished linguist, proposed that a kind of built-in system, the LAD or language acquisition device, must account for this complex intellectual achievement. (It should be understood that the device is not actually an organ but is merely an analogy.) As he formulates it:

Primary Linguistic Data $\longrightarrow$ LAD $\longrightarrow$ Grammar

That is, the language acquisition device receives primary linguistic data in the form of speech input from other people, and, by use of complex and little-known intellectual tools, the LAD constructs the grammar of the particular input language. The grammar is certainly not given in the input; nor can it be easily induced from the output by any means presently conceivable. It is clear that the human child is singularly well endowed to carry out this intellectual task.*

Most research in psycholinguistics has focused on the acquisition of grammar and syntax, but there is a mounting interest in problems of semantics, of what the child's speech *means*. The same simple combination of two words may have many different meanings; "Baby hat" used in different contexts can mean "That is the baby's hat" (pointing to a hat) or "Mommie is putting on my hat." The child intends to convey a range of meanings, but he cannot yet express these different meanings. Investigation of young children's speech in English, German, Russian, Finnish, Turkish, and Samoan suggests that

there is a striking uniformity across children and across languages in the kinds of meanings expressed in simple two-word utterances, suggesting that semantic development is closely tied to general cognitive development. The following range of semantic relations is typical of early child speech:

* D. I. Slobin, "On the Nature of Talk to Children," in *Foundations of Language Development: A Multidisciplinary Approach*, ed. Eric Lenneberg and Elizabeth Lenneberg (New York: UNESCO, in press).

IDENTIFICATION:	*see doggie*
LOCATION:	*book there*
REPETITION:	*more milk*
NONEXISTENCE:	*allgone thing*
NEGATION:	*not wolf*
POSSESSION:	*my candy*
ATTRIBUTION:	*big car*
AGENT-ACTION:	*mama walk*
ACTION-OBJECT:	*hit you*
AGENT-OBJECT:	*mama book*
ACTION-LOCATION:	*sit chair*
ACTION-RECIPIENT:	*give paper*
ACTION-INSTRUMENT:	*cut knife*
QUESTION:	*where ball?*

The universality of such a list is impressive.*

The Child's Thought

PREOPERATIONAL THOUGHT

As the child's language becomes more complex, new cognitive processes appear and intellectual skills increase. The second broad period of intellectual development according to Piaget is the *preoperational*, extending from approximately a year-and-a-half to seven years of age. Recall that at the end of the first period of cognitive development, the sensorimotor, the child manipulates objects and uses them as a means to attain his goals. However, all of his thinking and reasoning is limited to objects and events that are immediately present and directly perceived. In contrast, in the preoperational period, the child begins to use *mental symbols*—images or words—that stand for or *represent* objects that are not present. Simple examples are found in the child's play: his bicycle may be an airplane, a box becomes a house, and a piece of cloth is used as a robe. The use of symbols is also seen in *deferred imitation*, that is, imitation of a model that is no longer present. The following example of deferred imitation is taken from one of Piaget's observations of his daughter, when she was sixteen months old.

> [Jacqueline] had a visit from a little boy [of eighteen months] whom she used to see from time to time, and who, in the course of the afternoon, got into a terrible temper. He screamed as he tried to get out of a play-pen and pushed it backward, stamping his feet. J. stood watching him in amazement, never having witnessed such a scene before. The

* D. I. Slobin, "Seven Questions About Language Development," in *Psychology, 1972*, ed. P. C. Dodwell (London: Penguin, 1972).

next day, she herself screamed in her play-pen and tried to move it, stamping her foot lightly several times in succession.*

Since the model was not present at the time she copied his behavior, it may be inferred that Jacqueline had a mental representation of the tantrum and then based her behavior on this. Because she was able to symbolize the boy's action in this way, she could copy his behavior at a later time.

Piaget does not believe that the child's earliest use of words, during the sensorimotor period, is symbolic; rather, during this period words are concrete, intimately related to the child's ongoing activities or desires. During the preoperational period, however, the child gradually begins to use words to stand for absent objects and events. When she was twenty-three months old, Jacqueline returned from a trip and reported to her father that "Robert cry, ducks swim in lake, gone away." She was able to use words to stand for these past events.

According to Piaget, language plays a limited but important role in the formation of the child's thought, although language does not shape the child's mental activities.

Despite his new ability at language, the child often thinks nonverbally. He forms mental symbols which are based on imitation of things and not on their names. Language does, however, make a contribution. For example, when an adult uses a word which refers to a *class* of things, the child is given a glimpse at one facet of adult reasoning. An adult's language forces the child, to some degree, to consider the world from a new perspective. Nevertheless, it is probably fair to say that the child's thought depends less on his language than his language does on his thought. . . . The child interprets words in terms of his own personal system of meanings, and the child's meaning is not necessarily the same as the adult's. Although the culture provides the child with language, the latter does not immediately socialize the child's thought. In other words, language does not completely impose on the child the culturally desirable ways of thinking. Instead, the child distorts the language to fit his own mental structure. The child achieves mature thought only after a long process of development in which the role of language is but one contributing factor.†

During the early part of the preoperational stage, between the ages of approximately two and four, the child is egocentric, that is, centered about himself. He is unable to take another person's point of view. This is clearly seen in the child's speech and communication: he makes little

---

* J. Piaget, *Play, Dreams, and Imitation in Childhood* (New York: W. W. Norton & Company, 1962), p. 63.

† H. Ginsburg and S. Opper, *Piaget's Theory of Intellectual Development: An Introduction* (Englewood Cliffs, N.J.: Prentice-Hall, 1969), p. 85.

real effort to adapt what he says to the needs of the listener. The child's thought, too, is egocentric. As he sees it, the sun, moon, and clouds follow him around.

Children between two and four have no real conception of abstract principles that guide classification. If you present young children with a group of geometric shapes (for example, squares, circles, triangles, and stars) and ask them to "put together things that are alike," they do not use overall guiding principles in doing the task. Sometimes similarities determine what is put together; at other times, they group things on what appears to be a random basis—blue circles and yellow triangles or a red square and two blue circles. Children between the ages of five and seven produce real classes of objects, grouping them together on the basis of size, shape, or color. Yet even at this age the child cannot deal with what Piaget calls *class inclusion:* he cannot reason simultaneously about a part of the whole and the whole. For example, if you show a five-year-old ten red roses and five yellow roses and ask him whether there are more red roses or more roses, he is likely to reply that there are more red roses. When he deals with a subclass, the larger class is destroyed; he cannot conceive that a flower can belong to two classes at the same time.

Nor is the preoperational child able to handle problems of *ordering* or, as Piaget calls it, *seriating.* In one of Piaget's studies, children were given ten sticks that differed only in size. The child was asked to select the smallest stick. After this he was told, "Now try to put first the smallest, then one a bit bigger, than another a little bit bigger, and so on." Four-year-old children did not solve this problem successfully. Some of them made random arrangements, others ordered a few sticks but not all of them.

The concepts of the preoperational child and his understanding of situations are likely to be determined by his immediate perceptions, and often he perceives only a single salient aspect of a particular object or event. Ordinarily he will not relate different aspects or dimensions of a situation to one another. For example, in one experiment, a child is given two equal balls of clay and asked to roll one of them into a long sausage, or to flatten it into a pancake, or to break it into small pieces. Then he is asked whether the quantity of clay has increased, decreased, or remains equal. Most five- and six-year-olds think that a change in form necessarily produces a change in amount. Being able to take account of only one dimension (such as length) at a time, a child of this age is likely to report that the sausage contains more clay than the ball because it is longer.

Or in a parallel situation, a child is presented with two identical glasses, each of them containing the same amount of juice. After he agrees that each of the glasses contains the same amount of juice, the

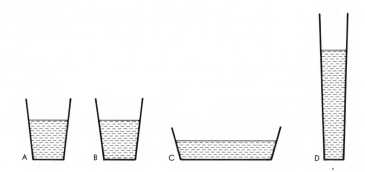

FIGURE 3.1. Conservation of continuous quantities.

liquid is poured from one glass into a third, shorter, wider glass. The column of liquid in the third glass is therefore shorter and wider than that in the other glass. The child is now asked whether the two glasses contain equal amounts. The preoperational child is likely to judge that the amount of liquid changes with the change in its appearance—for example, that there is more juice in the taller, thinner glass because the level of the liquid is higher in that glass. He does not yet realize that as the level of the liquid changes, there is a corresponding change in the width, which compensates for the change in level.

THE PERIOD OF CONCRETE OPERATIONS

The next broad period in cognitive development, *concrete operations*, begins at about seven years of age. During this period the deficiencies of the preoperational period are, to a large extent, overcome. The child acquires the concept of *conservation*, or what Piaget labels the *principle of invariance*. Faced with the questions about the amount of clay in the ball or sausage, or the amount of liquid in the glasses, the child understands that the amounts do not change just because the shape changes. He is likely to reason that "if you make the sausage into a ball again you see that nothing is added and nothing is taken away," or speaking of the liquid he may say that "what it gained in height it lost in width."

Furthermore, he acquires the concept of *reversibility*—the idea that, in thought, steps can be retraced, actions can be canceled, and the original situation can be restored. Thus, in making a sausage of a ball of clay, the diminution in the height of the ball is compensated for by the increase in length, so that the same quantity of clay is maintained. The number 2 can be squared to get 4, and extracting the square root of 4 yields 2. Using the concept of reversibility, the child can interrupt a sequence of steps in problem solving if he sees that he is not succeeding; and he can then return mentally to the beginning and start again.

The operational child succeeds in other tasks where preoperational children fail. He has a more advanced notion of classes in an abstract sense, and he can sort objects on the basis of such characteristics as shape, color, and size. He also understands *relationships*—for example, between classes and subclasses, recognizing that an object can belong to both simultaneously: white flowers are a subclass of flowers and a bouquet has more flowers than white flowers. While the preoperational child thinks in absolute terms—light or dark, big or small—and does not seem to understand relational terms, the child in the period of concrete operations thinks in terms of longer, higher, wider. He realizes that a brother must be the brother of someone, an object must be bigger or smaller—or to the right or left—compared with something else. When he is given a set of sticks, he can easily arrange them in order of size. The child's overall plan or strategy in classifying and seriating shows that he understands the *relationships* among his observations.

The cognitive achievements of the stage of concrete operations make the child's thought at this period much more solid and flexible than it was earlier. He is capable of elementary logical processes—or what Piaget calls *operations*—reasoning deductively, from premise to conclusion, in a logical way. But he does so only in limited and elementary ways, applying logic only to concrete events, perceptions, and representations of these. He does not think in abstract terms nor does he reason about verbal or hypothetical propositions. Thus, while the eight-, nine-, or ten-year-old has no trouble in ordering a series of dolls or sticks according to height, he has difficulty with verbal problems such as this one: "Edith is taller than Susan; Edith is shorter than Lilly; who is the tallest of the three?"

FORMAL OPERATIONS

Dealing with verbal expressions of logical relationships requires "formal operations" as distinct from "concrete operations," and children do not ordinarily use these until the age of eleven or twelve. In the view of Piaget and Inhelder, his chief collaborator, the application of logical rules and reasoning to abstract problems and propositions is the essence of mature intellectual ability. This final stage of intellectual development, the stage of formal operations, begins early in adolescence. The adolescent can reason deductively, making hypotheses about problem solutions, holding many variables in mind simultaneously. He is capable of scientific reasoning and of formal logic, and he can follow the *form* of an argument while disregarding its concrete content—hence the term *formal operations.*

In contrast with the operational child who is concerned only with concrete objects, perceptions, and representations of these, the adolescent seems preoccupied with thinking. He takes his own thought as an object and thinks about thinking, evaluating his own and other's logic, ideas, and thoughts. He considers general laws as well as real situations, and he is concerned with the hypothetically possible as well as reality. His dependence on the perception or manipulation of concrete objects is greatly reduced; he need no longer confine his attention to the immediate situation. By the time he is fifteen, the adolescent solves problems by analyzing them logically and formulating hypotheses about *possible* outcomes, about what *might* occur. The hypotheses may be complex ones involving many possible combinations of outcome. Nevertheless, the individual who has attained the stage of formal operations attempts to test his hypotheses either mentally or in reality by experiments.

The adolescent's ability to think scientifically is clearly illustrated by one experiment reported by Inhelder and Piaget. A subject is presented with five bottles of colorless liquid. The contents of bottle 1, 3, and 5, when combined, produce a brownish color; the fourth contains a color-reducing solution; and the second is neutral. The problem is to produce the brown solution. Adolescents in the stage of formal operations discover the solution little by little, by combining the various possibilities logically, and determining the effectiveness or neutrality of each liquid.

The Development of Intelligence

The discussion of Piaget's work in the preceding section focused on *qualitative* descriptions of the changes that occur as the child's cognitive abilities mature. In this approach, mental growth is viewed as a series of stages, a succession of new mental organizations or structures that are the foundations for the emergence of new mental abilities.

American psychologists have traditionally taken another, more quantitative, approach to the problem of mental growth. This is the *mental test* or *psychometric approach*, which stresses *individual differences* in intelligence and the factors underlying these differences. Intelligence is defined in terms of scores on a test, and intellectual growth is measured by the child's increasing ability to pass more items—and more difficult items—on an intelligence test as he grows older. There is little emphasis on the processes, or the components of mental ability, underlying changes in general ability.

Scores on intelligence tests are usually expressed in terms of an intelligence quotient or IQ, defined as the ratio between *mental age* (MA), which is a score based on performance on an intelligence test, and *chronological age*, multiplied by 100 ($IQ = MA/CA \times 100$). For example, if a seven-year-old has a mental age of 7, his IQ is 100 (average for the population at large). If he has a mental age of 6, his IQ is 85, which is generally considered in the "low average" range, falling in the lower 25 percent of the population. And if he has a mental age of 10, his IQ is $10/7 \times 100$ or 143, in the "very superior" range, the top 1 percent of the population. Only 3 percent of the population fall below IQ 70, the upper limit of the range of mental deficiency.

IQ scores have been used very widely in clinical evaluations, in educational counseling, and in school placement, because the score tells immediately where the individual ranks in brightness compared with others his own age. However, the use of intelligence tests with its emphasis on individual differences has recently raised a number of important social questions and become a source of major conflicts. One critical problem has to do with the use of intelligence tests with children from severely deprived, poverty backgrounds. Related to this are the issues of the heredity determinants of intelligence; race and socioeconomic differences in intellectual test performance; and the stability of the IQ over time (from early childhood to adolescence, for example). These are the issues to which we now turn.

THE NATURE OF THE INTELLIGENCE TEST

In defining intelligence, most testers—and psychologists who have constructed intelligence tests—stress the ability to think in abstract terms and to reason, together with the ability to use these functions for *adaptive purposes*. Piaget regards intelligence as a specific instance of *adaptive* behavior, of coping with the environment and organizing (and reorganizing) thought and action. All tests of intelligence contain items that tap the kinds of functions with which Piaget is concerned—problem solving, reasoning, abstract thinking. Almost all useful, valid intelligence tests are highly correlated with, and probably depend upon, facility in language; all aspects of language ability tend to be positively correlated with scores in intelligence tests.

Infant intelligence tests. Because infants' language abilities and intellectual competence are not well developed in the earliest years, it is difficult to assess their intelligence. Yet, for many reasons, it is highly useful to have such evaluations. Many parents are anxious to be assured that their babies are normal. If mental retardation or neurological deficiency can be diagnosed early, more effective counseling and guidance can be given parents. Valid early assessments of intelligence would also be of tremendous value in assigning orphan children to adoptive parents or in placing them in foster homes. Consequently, a number of infant tests have been developed. The most prominent and widely used of these tests, which consist primarily of perceptual and sensorimotor items, is the recently published Bayley Scales of Infant Development, which were developed after many years of intensive research. Table 1 lists some items from that test together with the age placements of these items (the average age at which babies can perform the task).

Unfortunately, such tests have only limited value. They may be useful in helping to diagnose gross mental deficiency, neurological defect, and specific disabilities in social responsiveness, vision, language, and hearing in young children. But they cannot predict a child's later intelligence; scores on these so-called intelligence tests given before eighteen months are absolutely worthless for the prediction of children's intellectual abilities when they are of school age.

Why is there so little correlation between the abilities measured by these infant tests and later intelligence? Most significantly, vastly different kinds of abilities are tapped at different ages. As a child's language becomes more highly developed and as his cognitive abilities improve, items involving these functions predominate in the tests, replacing the sensorimotor items of the infant scales. Items at the two- and three-year levels require more verbal ability and comprehension than the earlier tests, which test motor and sensory abilities almost exclusively.

Table 1

Examples of Infant Intelligence Test Items
from Bayley's Scales of Infant Development

ITEM	AGE PLACEMENT
	(MONTHS)
Responds to voice	0.7
Visually recognizes mother	2.0
Turns head to sound of rattle	3.9
Lifts cup with handle	5.8
Responds to verbal request (e.g., to wave bye-bye)	9.1
Imitates words	12.5
Uses gestures to make wants known	14.6
Imitates crayon stroke	17.8
Follows directions in pointing to parts of a doll	19.5
Uses two-word sentence	20.6
Points to three pictures	21.9
Names three objects shown to him	24.0

In the Stanford-Binet intelligence test, a widely used test for children, items are arranged according to the age levels at which the average child can pass them. Succeeding age levels throughout the preschool and school period include increased numbers of verbal items and more problem solving, reasoning, and abstract problems. To illustrate, the two-year-level items of this test include: identifying common objects, such as a cup, by their use; identifying major body parts; repeating two spoken digits; and placing simple blocks in a formboard. Among the four-year-level items are: naming pictures of a variety of common objects; recalling nine- and ten-word sentences; and correctly completing analogies (for instance, "In daytime it is light; at night it is . . ."). Completing a drawing of a man, copying a square, defining simple words, and counting four objects are five-year-level tasks. The eight-year-old tests involve: comprehending and answering questions about a short story; recognizing absurdities in stories; defining similarities and differences in pairs of objects (for example, a penny and a quarter); and general comprehension (What makes a sail boat move?) In short, as the tests show, as a child grows older he can master problems of increasing difficulty, which require of him greater verbal facility, comprehension, and problem-solving ability.

IQ stability and change. While the test scores of babies under eighteen months are not significantly predictive of later intelligence, IQs measured after that age tend to be more *stable*, that is, more highly correlated with scores attained in later childhood and adulthood. Table 2 reports correlation coefficients of intelligence test scores at various

Table 2

Correlations Between Intelligence Test Scores During the Preschool Years and IQ at Ages Ten and Eighteen

AGE	CORRELATION WITH IQ (STANFORD-BINET) AT AGE TEN	CORRELATION WITH IQ (WECHSLER) AT AGE EIGHTEEN
2	.37	.31
2½	.36	.24
3	.36	.35
4	.66	.42
6	.71	.61
8	.88	.70

SOURCE: M. P. Honzik, J. W. Macfarlane, and L. Allen, "The Stability of Mental Test Performance Between Two and Eighteen Years," *Journal of Experimental Education,* 17 (1948) no. 17:309–324.

early ages with scores at ages ten and eighteen years (young adulthood) based on a longitudinal study of 252 children. As the table shows, the predictive value of the test scores increases as the child matures. IQ at age six or seven is highly correlated with intelligence at ages ten and eighteen. This means that, in general, the child who is superior in intelligence at age six remains so, while the child who is inferior at this age generally scores low at later ages.

This does *not* mean that *every* individual standing is fixed; some children change markedly from one time to another. According to the data of one study, almost 60 percent of children change 20 or more points in IQ between the ages of six and eighteen, some improving rather consistently and some decreasing in IQ as they grow older. Such changes are, in many cases, related to personality traits and motivation, as the following case history of a subject in a longitudinal study illustrates. The boy's IQ fluctuated between 113 and 163 during his school years, the scores varying with his general state of health, psychological adjustment, and home conditions. At the age of six, when his Stanford-Binet IQ was at its lowest, he had chronic sinus trouble, bronchial asthma, and was in bed twelve weeks. His father contracted tuberculosis and his mother had to go to work; these changes produced a vast reorganization at home. The school reports at this time noted that the boy was restless, sensitive, and shy. In contrast, at age ten, when he scored 163, his father had recovered and was working again after a period of unemployment, his school adjustment had improved tremendously, and he was said to manifest "marvelous concentration" at school.

A systematic study of the personality correlates of IQ changes compared the thirty-five children in a longitudinal study who showed the greatest increase in IQ between the ages of six and ten with the thirty-five who showed the greatest decreases during this period. In comparison with the latter, it was found, the former were more interested in school work, studied harder, and were more strongly motivated to master intellectual problems. In general, they were more oriented toward achievement, and their mothers had encouraged them, since early childhood, to master problems of all sorts. Apparently, intelligence test performance to some extent reflects strength of motivation for achievement and for problem mastery. We may infer that altering this motivation may increase or decrease intelligence test scores during the school years; we shall return to this argument later (see p. 42).

By and large, scores on intelligence tests taken during early school years are good predictors of grammar school grades in reading, arithmetic, composition, spelling, and social studies, and they are also fairly good predictors of academic success in high school and college.

FACTORS RELATED TO PERFORMANCE
ON INTELLIGENCE TESTS

Intelligence tests do not yield "pure" measures of native ability or intellectual potential; they measure and evaluate performance in specific tasks—mostly, though not entirely, of a verbal kind. This kind of performance can be influenced by many factors—in fact, by practically all the factors that help shape psychological development. Both hereditary (genetic) and environmental factors affect individual performance, but it is impossible to determine the relative proportions of an individual's intelligence test scores that are attributable to the two sets of factors. Suppose, for example, a lower-class child whose parents are illiterate immigrants achieves a low score in an intelligence test. This score *may* be due to poor hereditary intellectual endowment. On the other hand, it *may* be the outcome of his impoverished background, lack of intellectual stimulation in his home, inadequate verbal ability (at least in English)— or any number of other factors or combinations of factors. We shall discuss such factors in greater detail below. Here it is important to note that knowledge of a person's score in itself tells us nothing about the reasons that he achieves that score.

Genetic influences on intelligence. Psychologists generally accept the notion that heredity contributes to intellectual ability and probably sets the limits of this ability. But they would not agree that an individual's intelligence is genetically established at conception, and is therefore fixed and unchanging. The limits that heredity sets are flexible ones.

Several kinds of evidence support the view that genetic factors contribute to the determination of intelligence as measured by test performance. In one type of study, two kinds of correlations are compared: (1) the correlation between IQ scores of children raised by their own parents and the parents' scores; and (2) the correlation between the intelligence test scores of foster children adopted in infancy with those of their foster parents. The correlation between the IQs of parents and their natural children has generally been found to be about .50, while the correlation between the IQs of foster parents and their adopted children is, in most studies, about .20. Apparently, children resemble their true parents in intelligence test performance to a significantly greater degree than foster children resemble foster parents. Presumably, heredity accounts for the greater correlation between true parents and their children, especially since the foster children studied were adopted very early in life.

Further impressive evidence on the role of heredity in intelligence comes from comparing correlations of the intelligence test scores of *identical* twins (who develop from a single fertilized egg and thus have exactly the same genetic constitutions) and those of fraternal twins (who develop from two fertilized eggs and hence differ genetically). The IQs of identical twins correlate very highly, about .90 on the average, while the IQs of fraternal twins correlate about .55. In other words, identical twins score very much alike on intelligence tests, and this holds true even if they were reared in quite different environments and were exposed to different experiences. In fact, the correlation between the IQs of identical twins *reared apart* was .76, while the IQs of fraternal twins who had been raised in the *same environment* correlated .55. In other words, despite being reared in vastly different environments, identical twins were more alike in tested intelligence than fraternal twins who had been raised in the same environment. Obviously, heredity must be a major determinant of intelligence, helping to set the limits within which the environment may affect a child's intelligence test score.

Nevertheless, it should be noted that even among the identical twins environmental factors had some impact on performance. The greater the differences in their environmental experiences, the more divergent were the identical twins' IQs. For example, one of a pair of identical twin girls spent a considerable part of her elementary school years in an isolated mountain setting where there were no schools. She dropped out of school entirely when very young. Her twin sister, adopted into a home where there was much emphasis on education and accomplishment, was intellectually stimulated, particularly by her foster mother. The Stanford-Binet IQ of the first girl was 92; that of the second 116, a difference of 24 points, and the latter was almost seven years more advanced than her sister in educational achievement.

Environmental influences on intelligence.   Clearly, then, environmental, motivational, and personality factors—including nutrition, intellectual stimulation, and achievement orientation in the home—also contribute significantly to intelligence. For example, anxious, fearful children have difficulty concentrating on academic and problem-solving tasks and are likely to perform poorly on intelligence tests. On the average, children of school age—particularly boys—with high scores on tests of anxiety have somewhat lower intelligence test scores than their peers who have relatively little anxiety. Children with low self-esteem who feel personally inadequate and inferior—perhaps because they are poor or black (or both)—will give up too easily in the test situation and thus perform poorly. Furthermore, children who come from deprived backgrounds probably have few role models who have used intellectual skills and education to "get ahead"; hence they are not likely to be motivated for intellectual achievement or for high-level performance on tests of cognitive functioning.

The tremendous impacts of broad, general environmental factors have been called to the psychologists' attention in rather dramatic ways by findings on social-class and race differences in intelligence test performance. Children of the upper and middle classes consistently score better than those of the lower class in intelligence tests, the average difference between the highest and the lowest social classes being about 20 IQ points. And black school children score on the average 10 to 15 points below their white schoolmates on most standard tests of intelligence.

Some psychologists have interpreted these class and race differences as evidence of the hereditary determination of intelligence—that is, perhaps the upper classes and whites are of superior intellectual endowment and transmit this genetically to their children. However, most psychologists argue that IQ differences between racial and class groups can readily be explained in terms of environmental and experiential, rather than genetic, factors. Certainly, on the average middle-class whites and poor blacks live in vastly different environments and have different backgrounds of experience.

Many kinds of environmental factors affect intellectual functioning. For example, inadequate nutrition during a mother's pregnancy—especially protein deficiency—can have enduring adverse effects on her child's intellectual ability. Lower-class persons are more likely than others to have inadequate diets and, consequently, to produce children of inferior intellectual ability. Some of the observed social-class and race differences in test performance may be due to such nutritional factors.

Furthermore, the contents of intelligence tests draw much more heavily on the experiences and interests of middle-class whites than of other groups. Therefore, the items of the test may be much less interesting and less meaningful to children from other social and racial groups. This, too, may help account for the apparent cognitive deficiencies of economically deprived and black children.

Of greatest importance in explaining these differences in intelligence test performance is the fact that there are social-class and cultural differences in early child rearing. Specifically, economically deprived families provide restricted experiences and little intellectual or cultural stimulation for their young children. A number of prominent psychologists have argued persuasively that intellectual interests and the motivation for intellectual competence are formed during early childhood and are very vulnerable at this period. The infant needs opportunities for learning and he needs to confront various kinds of stimulation if he is to become intellectually motivated and alert. Deprivation of cognitive and social stimulation early in life may produce irreversible adverse effects, according to some. For optimal intellectual development the child needs to have interesting, stimulating, and pleasurable experiences, beginning in very early infancy.

Poor children, both white and black, enter school with an initial disadvantage; that is, by the time they enter school they perform more poorly on cognitive tasks and tests of intelligence, on the average, than middle-class white children. And, sadly, they frequently suffer a kind of "progressive" retardation, falling further and further behind in intellectual functioning as they go through school. This presents a problem of acute social importance. As a culture we are committed to drastic reduction of social, economic, and educational inequalities between social and racial groups. Can these cognitive handicaps that are manifested relatively early in life be overcome?

Reducing early cognitive deficiencies. If early environmental stimulation is an important antecedent of subsequent intellectual functioning, it should be possible to raise the level of a child's intelligence by providing him with more stimulation early in his life. In fact, there have been many attempts to overcome cognitive deficiencies by nursery school training. These educational efforts have not always been successful, unfortunately, for the problem of raising a child's intellectual level is not a simple one. Clearly, merely placing a disadvantaged child in a nursery school and exposing him to the usual nursery school program will not in itself produce increments in cognitive skills. But special, intensive individual attention and training—especially if these involve the mother as well as the nursery school teacher—may have significant positive results in overcoming some of the adverse effects of early deprivation. We cannot review all the important investigations of compensatory education here; what follows is a sample of relevant studies that indicate the range of programs attempted and their fruitfulness.

In the Early Training Project directed by Susan Grey and Rupert Klaus at George Peabody College in Nashville, Tennessee, the subjects were black preschool children from poverty families in the South. Experimental groups of children attended two or three special summer sessions of preschools that had programs stressing motivation toward achievement. At the same time, the training was designed to foster the development of characteristics that are important in school success—persistence, ability to delay gratification, and interest in schoolwork. Specially trained black teachers worked with the mothers of these children, meeting with them weekly, making them aware of children's motives, and encouraging them to reward the child's accomplishments. Control children from the same social and economic background did not attend preschool or receive any special training.

At the end of the training period, the children who had attended preschool were markedly superior to the controls in a number of cognitive tests, including tests of intelligence, vocabulary, language ability, and reading readiness. Follow-up studies of these subjects yielded modest but encouraging results. After twenty-seven months, the experimental subjects had maintained their gains, and after five years, when the children had finished two years of public school, the positive effects of early training were still apparent. The controls showed the usual phenomenon of progressive retardation. These results suggest that it is possible to create programs that have lasting positive effects; but the programs must start when children are very young and must provide a program specifically planned in accordance with the deficits to be expected in such children.

Special, intensive tutoring of nursery school children from disadvantaged backgrounds may be effective; even if it is not accompanied by intensive work with mothers. In one excellent study, twenty-two nursery school children were given daily individual tutoring sessions lasting between fifteen and twenty minutes and conducted by trained nursery school teachers. During the sessions the children were encouraged to become actively involved in cognitive tasks and to "organize thoughts, . . . reflect upon situations, comprehend the meaning of events and . . . structure behavior so as to be able to choose among alternatives." The teacher took advantage of every opportunity to aid the child in developing his budding ability to think and to reflect. The study lasted four months and all subjects were tested before and after the training period.

The average gain in IQ for the group that had five days of tutoring each week was 15 points, and the group that had three days of tutoring per week gained an average of 7 points. In contrast, children in the control groups did not gain in intelligence on the average. Incidentally, many of the children in the tutored groups showed rather dramatic changes in behavior, becoming less withdrawn, more coherent, less anxious. Clearly, individual tutoring oriented toward actively involving the child in cognitive tasks can be effective. The procedure is, of course, expensive, but the tremendous social benefits that result may be worth the cost.

If the deficiencies in cognitive functioning among poor and disadvantaged children are related to inadequate stimulation in the very early years, even in infancy, shouldn't special efforts begin even earlier than the preschool period? Will increasing the level of environmental stimulation during infancy enhance later cognitive functioning? There is some evidence that this effect can be achieved by concerted efforts. In one study, eight college-educated women were trained to tutor black infants in poverty areas in their homes. The individualized training sessions began when the infants were fourteen months of age and lasted twenty-one months. During this period, each infant was tutored an hour a day four times a week. Tutors concentrated on verbal stimulation, using books, toys, and anything else available to maintain the infant's interest. The tutored infants had gained 17 IQ points on the average—significantly more than their untutored controls—when they were tested at thirty-six months of age. The twenty-one-month period of tutoring had some very worthwhile effects, although it is not known whether these are enduring.

In an even more ambitious project, one psychologist taught women with modest educational backgrounds how to tutor mothers of infants who would ordinarily be expected to develop rather poorly intellectually. Mothers were taught to play "learning games" with their children involving sensorimotor activities, labeling objects with words, noting the differences between objects, and pointing to things. The purpose of the games was to help mothers become more sensitive to their infants' needs and abilities and, at the same time, to encourage them to devote more time and attention to training and enjoying the baby. The preliminary results were encouraging, especially for female infants; for the girls there was a 6-point overall gain on infant scales, and boys made smaller gains.

These few programs, well conceived and carried out, appear to have made some changes; at least in some cases, these changes are lasting ones. However, it must be carefully noted that the positive results did not follow simply from attendance at nursery school. Rather, the changes came from intensive, individualized work with the children, based on their needs, interests, and abilities. In many cases, participation by mothers was of paramount importance. These are expensive programs, and they cannot be carried out superficially; yet from the points of view of both the individual and society, the results may well be worth the expense and the effort.

Personality Development

I: BIOLOGICAL AND CULTURAL INFLUENCES

chapter four

Personality is a broad and comprehensive concept that refers to the organization of an individual's predispositions and his unique adjustments to his environment. Personal characteristics (or traits), emotions, motivations, values, goals, and ways of perceiving are all aspects of personality structure.

Personality development is an enormously complicated process, shaped by a vast number of interrelated and continually interacting factors. At least four broad types of factors play a role in determining a child's personality characteristics and behavior. The first type is *biological* and includes genetic endowment, temperament, physical appearance, and rate of maturation. The second major category is *cultural-group membership.* Each culture has a "typical" personality—a particular pattern of motives, goals, ideals, and values—which is characteristic and distinctive of that culture and which children growing up in that culture acquire. The Japanese are generally more "group oriented" and interdependent in their relations with other people, self-effacing, and passive; Americans are more independent, self-assertive, and aggressive. Obviously, children in Japanese and American cultures are brought up in different ways to achieve these cultural differences in personality. Analogously, within the American scene, many Zuñi Indian children, reared in traditional ways

—many of them on reservations—are trained to be cooperative and equalitarian, uninterested in personal aggrandizement and achievement. In contrast, American middle-class parents are likely to foster the development of achievement motivation in their children.

A third and perhaps the most critical factor in personality development is the individual's *unique history of experiences with others*. Personality is largely a product of social learning, and the child's social interactions provide his fundamental learning experiences. Relationships with other members of his family and of his social-class, ethnic, and religious groups are of outstanding significance.

The fourth type of influence on overt behavior and personality characteristics is the *situation*, that is, the stimuli directly impinging on the individual at any particular time. The other people present, the child's feelings of the moment (for instance, fatigue, frustration, anxiety, calm, or a happy mood), and the immediate rewards and punishments offered —all of these affect the personality characteristics and predispositions he will manifest. An extremely active, noisy, jumpy child readily learns to be quieter and more restrained in the schoolroom if he has a strict teacher. When the child encounters new situations in which his habitual reactions and patterns of response are not acceptable, he will try new and different behavior. If these new responses are rewarded, his characteristic responses may be modified substantially. This fact underlies the use of the techniques of behavior therapy which we shall discuss later (see pp. 88–89).

All these forces are interwoven—operating, interacting, and affecting personality development concurrently. Thus, although a child's cultural-group membership and his relationships with his parents are central in shaping his personality and behavior, their effects may be tempered by his energy and activity levels, which are, at least partially, biologically determined.

It is only for convenience of exposition that in the following discussion of personality development we focus on important biological and social forces one at a time. In actuality, it is often difficult to separate the effects of one determinant from those of another. Moreover, our knowledge is still very limited. The solutions to many problems in personality development—such as the relative impacts of various biological, social, and situational factors—await further scientific research.

Biological Factors

GENETIC INFLUENCES ON PERSONALITY AND BEHAVIOR

As we noted earlier, it is almost impossible to separate hereditary and environmental influences on human behavior, because every manifest characteristic or trait is a product of complex interactions between genetically determined potentialities and environmental forces. However, there is solid experimental evidence that certain characteristics of dogs and other animals, such as aggressiveness, nervousness, timidity, sociability, and trainability—are strongly influenced by genetic endowment. Selective breeding can produce litters of mild, calm dogs or nervous, aggressive ones. Cocker spaniels are easy to train, relatively unemotional, and exhibit little fear, while beagles and terriers are difficult to train and more fearful.

Are comparable characteristics in humans transmitted genetically? While intelligence is to some extent under genetic control (see pp. 43–44), the role of hereditary endowment in determining other aspects of psychological functioning is not so clear. Some features of personality appear to be influenced at least indirectly by these factors. For example, intensive longitudinal observations of a large group of infants, extending from the age of two or three months old until two years, indicate that certain "intrinsic reaction types," manifested very early, are apt to persist. The variables constituting these "types" include activity or passivity, intensity of reaction, approach or withdrawal tendencies, positive or negative moods, distractibility, and regularity or irregularity. It is impossible to determine whether these enduring patterns are genetically determined or learned very early, but the investigators are convinced that these are, in fact, innate and unlearned—some children, they feel, are endowed with greater tendencies toward, say, activity, distractability, and stronger reactions than others.

Other findings suggest that tendencies toward inhibition and social introversion or their opposites may also be partially under genetic control; identical twins are more similar to each other than fraternal twins in these traits. As infants, identical twins are more alike than fraternal twins in tendencies to smile and to show fear of strangers. Findings consistent with these come from studies of high school students who responded to personality questionnaires. Identical twins resembled each other much more than fraternal twins in measures of introversion-extroversion, aggressiveness, moodiness, dependency, and shyness. This strongly suggests that heredity contributes to the development of these characteristics.

Some mental disorders appear to have genetic components. There is evidence that this is true of schizophrenia, a profound psychosis characterized by severe impairments in logical thinking and in emotional relationships with others, loss of contact with reality and marked withdrawal. An investigator examined thousands of records of schizophrenic patients to determine how many of them had twin siblings, either identical or fraternal. Then he determined whether or not the other twin was also schizophrenic. Among the identical twins this occurred in 86 percent of the cases, among the fraternals in only 15 percent of the cases. Such a large difference between the two kinds of twins indicates that genetic factors contribute to the development of this emotional disorder, but the data should not be interpreted to mean that schizophrenia is directly inherited. Rather, there appears to be a genetic *predisposition* to respond to strong environmental stress with schizophrenic reactions; if the individual with this predisposition is exposed to the appropriate environmental conditions, he is more likely to become schizophrenic than someone not so predisposed.

Some mental illnesses of childhood *may* have a genetic basis, although the evidence is not clearcut. For example, the *autistic child* is "different" from the very first days of life, avoiding contact, forming no relationships with others—no social smiles, no recognition of family members, no social games. He seems lonely and isolated. His language and speech are distorted and often unintelligible, and not ordinarily used for communication with others.

Autism can be differentiated from *childhood schizophrenia*, which generally does not develop until the child is about five or six years of age. Ordinarily, the schizophrenic child speaks, while the autistic one does not. Many authorities maintain that both of these childhood mental illnesses have strong genetic components, but it is impossible to assess the genetic contributions precisely or to specify the genetic mechanisms involved in the transmission of these illnesses.

INFLUENCES OF PHYSICAL APPEARANCE
AND PHYSIQUE

Physical appearance—structure of the face, height, weight, body proportions—is to a large extent genetically determined, and, as everyone knows, physical appearance and physique may significantly affect personality and behavior. We all know of people who because of physical attractiveness achieve goals or positions they might not otherwise have attained, or who because of ugliness or deformity become profoundly unhappy, shy, or withdrawn. In the world of young boys, physical strength and prowess bring prestige and success. Those who are advanced in development, tall and muscular for their age, are more likely to be self-confident, outgoing leaders. Furthermore, these boys are likely to mature faster and have earlier growth spurts than others, so they are in a good position to continue their predominance. Lanky boys with relatively poor muscular development are less likely to be able to hold their own in sports or rough-and-tumble play. Furthermore, these boys tend to mature more slowly, so they see others surpass them in size and athletic skill, and perhaps in social development, during early adolescence. This experience is likely to reinforce early-established negative self-concepts.

Of course, these effects may be exaggerated or mitigated by other factors that affect personality development. The tall, well-built, strong boy is not likely to become secure and self-confident if he happens to be unintelligent and unsuccessful in school, or if as a result of his relationships at home he is insecure and dependent. On the other hand, if the weak, unattractive boy is bright and academically successful, or has stable, reassuring relationships at home, he may not become insecure in spite of the fact that his physical appearance initially arouses unfavorable reactions from his peers.

Systematic studies of normal children show that there are small but significant relationships between body build and personality. According to the data of one study of ten- and eleven-year-olds, small, poorly coordinated, and relatively weak children are inclined to be timid, fearful, passive, and generally worried. In contrast, tall, strong, energetic, well-coordinated children of the same age are playful, self-expressive, talkative, productive, and creative.

It hardly seems likely that the genetic or constitutional factors that help determine physical characteristics also influence personality traits directly. Rather, some features of physique may affect the individual's capabilities, aptitudes, and interests; most critically, peers' and adults' reactions to the child are affected by his appearance, build, and strength. To illustrate, in our culture peers and adults are likely to react to a small, awkward, physically weak child as though he were delicate, sensitive, dependent, unaggressive, and perhaps lacking in competence. Furthermore, since this child is not likely to be successful in physical games and athletics, he is not likely to develop intense interests in these activities and may begin to withdraw from others, as well as from physical activities. Not surprisingly, he may become timid, passive, and dependent.

Tall, strong, well-coordinated children, on the other hand, are likely to be considered more mature, independent, aggressive, and competent. In addition, these children are likely to be skillful in motor activities, successful in athletics, and energetic in social interactions. For these reasons they may be accorded high social status, and may therefore develop self-confidence and outgoing characteristics. In sum, a child's physical characteristics may affect his approach to the social environment, the expectancies of others, and their reactions to him. These, in turn, may have impacts on personality development.

RATE OF MATURATION

As we learned earlier, there are striking variations in the age at which adolescents reach physical maturity. Relatively mature and immature adolescents of the same age are undoubtedly exposed to different social-psychological environments. A late-maturing boy looks younger than his age and is likely to be regarded and treated as immature by others. He may sometimes doubt whether his body will ever develop properly and whether he will be as well endowed sexually as others he sees developing around him.

The early-maturing boy, on the other hand, clearly sees his own growth and his own physical changes leading to adulthood. Others regard him as more grown up socially and emotionally, and he has an advantage over the late-maturing boy in competitive athletics, which continue to be important at this age.

The psychological consequences of these differences have been demonstrated in studies comparing the personalities of late- and early-maturing adolescent boys. Those who are relatively retarded physically tend to reveal more maladjustment. They have some negative self-concepts, harbor stronger feelings of inadequacy and rejection, and are both more dependent and more rebellious. In contrast, the early-maturing boys generally feel adequate, accepted by others, self-confident, independent, mature, and capable of playing an adult role; apparently, these boys are more likely than the others to live in circumstances that are conducive to good psychological adjustment.

Among girls, early maturing—at the age of eleven or twelve—may be a slight handicap socially. Some girls are embarrassed by their early maturation. But beginning with the seventh grade, and throughout the junior high school years, early maturing becomes a social advantage and is associated with being popular and highly regarded by peers. The findings about the effects of early and late maturing must be interpreted cautiously, however, for

> although rate of maturing and associated factors may affect personality development, the relationship between physical status and psychological characteristics is by no means simple. A vast number of complex, interacting factors, including rate of maturation, determine each adolescent's unique personality structure. Hence, in any specific instance, the *group* findings . . . may not be directly applicable, for other physical, psychological, or social factors may attenuate the effects of late- or early-maturing. For example, an adolescent boy who is fundamentally secure and has warm, accepting parents and generally rewarding social relationships may not develop strong feelings of inadequacy even if he matures slowly. Analogously, the early-maturing boy who has deep feelings of insecurity, for whatever reasons, will probably not gain self-confidence simply because he matures early. In summary, in understanding any individual case, generalizations based on [these] data . . . must be particularized in the light of the individual's past history and present circumstances.*

* P. H. Mussen and M. C. Jones, "Self-Conceptions, Motivations, and Interpersonal Attitudes of Late- and Early-Maturing Boys," *Child Development* 28 (June 1957): 255.

Socialization and Cultural Influences
on Personality

From the point of view of personality development, the most significant aspect of a child's world is his *social* environment. Virtually all human beings live in a society, an interacting group of people. And each society has a distinctive culture, a body of stored knowledge, characteristic ways of thinking and feeling, attitudes, goals, and ideals.

"Culture regulates our lives at every turn. From the moment we are born until we die there is, whether we are conscious of it or not, constant pressure upon us to follow certain types of behavior that other men have created for us."* An individual's biological heritage is directly or indirectly influential in the development of his personality, but cultural factors play an overriding role, as the following story—told by the late Clyde Kluckhohn, famous Harvard anthropologist—illustrates:

> Some years ago I met in New York City a young man who did not speak a word of English and was obviously bewildered by American ways. By "blood" he was as American as you or I, for his parents had gone from Indiana to China as missionaries. Orphaned in infancy, he was reared by a Chinese family in a remote village. All who met him found him more Chinese than American. The facts of his blue eyes and light hair were less impressive than a Chinese style of gait, Chinese arm and hand movements, Chinese facial expression, and Chinese modes of thought. The biological heritage was American, but the cultural training had been Chinese.†

How does an individual's cultural-group membership influence the development of his personality? Primarily by prescribing—and limiting —what a child will be taught and what he will learn. As we shall demonstrate, each culture expects, and trains, its members to behave in the ways that are acceptable to the group. To a marked degree, the child's cultural group defines the range of experiences and situations he is likely to encounter and the values and personality characteristics that will be reinforced and hence learned. Each culture has its own concepts and specific techniques of child rearing, as well as a set of expectations regarding patterns of approved behavior.

SOCIALIZATION

Socialization is the process by which an individual acquires, from the enormously wide range of behavioral potentialities that are open to him

* Clyde Kluckhohn, *Mirror for Man* (New York: McGraw-Hill, 1949), p. 327.
† Ibid., pp. 320–21.

at birth, those behavior patterns that are customary and acceptable according to the standards of his family and social group. Within the limits set by his hereditary endowments and abilities, a child in a complex and varied culture can become almost any type of person: aggressive or mild, competitive or cooperative, meat-eating or vegetarian, motivated toward or uninterested in intellectual achievement, sexually expressive or inhibited, dependent or independent, honest or dishonest, politically liberal or reactionary. The possibilities are, in effect, almost infinite; yet ordinarily, any individual adopts only the behavior deemed appropriate for his own social, ethnic, and religious groups. How this occurs—how the individual acquires behavior characteristics congruent with the values and standards of his own group—is the core problem in studying the process of socialization.

The culture in which the child grows up prescribes, to a considerable degree, the *methods* and *goals* of socialization—that is, *how* he will be trained and *which* personality characteristics, motives, attitudes, and values he will adopt. There are, of course, universal aspects of socialization; every culture makes provisions for maintaining and perpetuating itself, for establishing an orderly way of life, and for satisfying the biological needs of its members. In all cultures, children must be fed, toilet trained, and protected from illness. No culture can survive and endure unless aggressive and sexual impulses and dependency are to some extent controlled, although cultures differ widely in their permissiveness (or restrictiveness) of expression of these motives.

There are numberless variations in the methods cultures use for achieving these and other important goals. In some cultures, infants are always handled gently and their needs are met promptly and completely, whereas in other cultures the infant is frequently and severely frustrated. Most American babies are breast-fed for only a few months, but in some African cultures infants are permitted to nurse until they are five or six years old. The culture may prescribe that toilet training be accomplished gradually, or babies may be expected to achieve bladder and bowel control by the age of six months and punished if they have accidents after that. Of course, every culture's ways of handling child rearing have a specific goal: facilitating the acquisition of culturally approved patterns of personality characteristics, motivation, attitudes, and values—in other words, producing individuals with personality structures that will fit into the culture and help maintain it.

Training to accomplish these goals begins very early. For example, within the first three months the Japanese infant starts his training to become group-oriented, interdependent in his relationships with others, and passive, while the American baby begins to learn independence and self-assertion. American mothers are more lively and stimulating in their approaches to their babies, moving them about, looking at them, and vocalizing more in attempts to excite their interests. Japanese mothers, in contrast, spend more time with their babies in general, talk with them to soothe them when they are fussy, and have a generally quieting approach toward their babies. By the age of three or four months, the infants already respond in culturally appropriate ways.

> The Japanese boy baby seems passive, and he lies quietly with occasional unhappy vocalizations, while his mother, in her care, does more lulling, carrying, and rocking of her baby. She seems to try to soothe and quiet the child and to communicate with him physically rather than verbally. On the other hand, the American infant is more active, happily vocal, and exploring of his environment, and his mother in her care does more looking at and chatting to her baby. She seems to stimulate the baby to activity and to vocal response. It is as if the American mother wanted to have a vocal, active baby, and the Japanese mother wanted to have a quiet, contented baby. In terms of the styles of caretaking of the mothers in the two cultures, they seem to get what they apparently want.*

Later training for the culturally approved patterns of behavior and social interrelationships is generally consistent with the earliest training given by parents, even though it may be given by others—by older brothers and sisters, relatives, teachers, or religious leaders. Thus, in Japan the child's later experiences lead toward increasing interdependence in social relationships, while the American path very early leads toward increasing independence from others. Thus, in the American family the child is likely to be separated from the family in sleeping arrangements within the first few years of life, while the Japanese child continues to sleep with his parents during the transition from infancy to childhood, and after that time he is very likely to sleep with a brother or sister until approximately the age of fifteen.

Throughout their childhood, American children are encouraged to be self-reliant and independent and at the same time to deny feelings of dependency. Asking for help may provoke anxiety or feelings of inadequacy in American children and adolescents. In traditional Chinese culture, on the other hand, independence is not so highly prized, and asking for help is not so likely to produce feelings of inferiority.

General American culture—middle-class American culture in particular—stresses competition and personal achievement. Early in life, American children are made aware of the value of accomplishment, and

* W. Caudill and H. Weinstein, "Maternal Care and Infant Behavior in Japan and America," in *Readings in Child Behavior and Development*, 3rd ed., ed. C. S. Lavatelli and F. Stendler (New York: Harcourt Brace Jovanovich, 1972), p. 84.

as they grow older rewards for competition increase and competitive attitudes become stronger. In contrast, sharing and cooperation are stressed by the Hopi Indians and on Israeli kibbutzim (collective farms), and children in these cultures are discouraged from competing. In American schoolrooms, competition has traditionally been a powerful motive for doing good work rapidly and efficiently, while among the Hopi children who complete their work quickly are likely to "hold back," for they are reluctant to embarrass others. White Americans are likely to strive to achieve "leading" positions in school or community, but Hopi children refuse such honors, preferring to remain equal, but not superior, to their peers.

ADOLESCENCE IN DIFFERENT CULTURES

In some societies, such as our own, the transition from childhood to adulthood is relatively abrupt and difficult. Many new tasks must be learned rapidly and new responses acquired within a very short period of time. American culture demands that the adolescent resolve many problems simultaneously—achieving some independence from his family; choosing and preparing for a vocation; and making a mature, heterosexual adjustment, including setting up a separate household. The culture insists that the adolescent cope with all these problems, even though he may wish to remain secure, dependent, and free of responsibility. Under the circumstances, it is not surprising that in our culture adolescence is often a period of stress, conflict, and emotional upset.

In other societies the child prepares much more gradually for independence, for his vocational role, and for mature sexuality. Among the Indians of Mexico, for example, young children are treated with great leniency and have few assigned duties, but they soon begin to take on some of the necessary work of the community. By the age of six or seven, the typical Mexican Indian girl begins to care for her younger brothers and sisters, goes to the market, and helps serve food and wash dishes. Boys of the same age begin to help gather food in the fields and to care for large animals such as goats and donkeys. Gradually they take increasing responsibility and perform the work they will assume as adults. Parents are nurturant and do not pressure their children to do jobs beyond their capabilities, but they expect them to do some basic work they are capable of doing. In Mexican Indian Culture, adolescence is not likely to be a period of stress or conflict.

Adjustment to mature sexuality is also conditioned by cultural factors. Traditionally, American middle-class sex training has been highly restrictive; children and adolescents are supposed to inhibit sexual responses, including even thoughts about sex. Yet adults are supposed to reverse these early-established attitudes suddenly and to enjoy sexual activity after they are married. As a result, conflicts about sex are common in our culture; early learning of sexual inhibition and anxiety about sex may be very difficult to overcome.

Many other cultures have much more permissive attitudes toward sexual activity among children and adolescents. In some societies, sexual experience is approved and even encouraged from early childhood on. In one African group, for example, children are expected to prepare for adult life and mature sexual functions. From the age of nine or ten children in this society build little huts outside the village and, with the complete approval of their parents, boys and girls play at being husband and wife. These boy-girl sexual relationships may extend into adolescence, although there are often exchanges of partners until marriage. In societies such as these there are few problems of adult sexual adjustment.

The qualities of the sexual relationships also reflect general social orientation of the culture. Among the Zuñi there is an emphasis on pleasant, cooperative human relationships, unmarred by feelings of guilt. Consequently, Zuñi sexual relationships are cooperative rather than competitive or exploitative. In contrast, among the Mundugamor of New Guinea, aggression and competition play an important part in sexual relationships, for these motives are integral features of the Mundugamor way of life.

SOCIAL-CLASS DIFFERENCES

American culture is not an undifferentiated entity; ours is a complex, differentiated, pluralistic society, stratified along ethnic and socioeconomic lines (with many social inequalities related to this stratification) and undergoing rapid change. Each ethnic and socioeconomic group has its own distinct culture, philosophy of life, system of values, and patterns of behavior. Children in different segments of American society have different child-rearing experiences, different opportunities, and different rewards, and consequently they differ in personality structure, behavior, and attitudes.

By the time they enter school, children are keenly aware of class distinctions and of their own relative positions in the social hierarchy. Personality tests reveal that black children and lower-class whites are lower in self-esteem and self-assurance than white middle-class children. Furthermore, lower-class children, particularly blacks, have much less sense of personal efficacy. They are much less inclined than middle-class children to believe that their own actions determine what happens to them; rather, they see their lives as controlled by external events.

Physical aggression seems to play a larger part in the lives of lower-class people than in those of middle-class people; lower-class children have generally been found to be more physically aggressive and belligerent than those of the middle class. Sexual expression is also less inhibited in the lower class and many more lower-class than middle-class adolescents have sexual intercourse.

A middle-class child's tendency to inhibit aggression and sexual expression along with his high achievement motivation may be considered manifestations of a general middle-class emphasis on "delay of gratification," that is, on the importance of sacrificing immediate goals to obtain more substantial long-term objectives. In studies in which children must choose between the alternatives of a small immediate reward (say, a small amount of candy) and a larger delayed reward (say, a large candy bar the next day), both black and white lower-class children tend to choose the first alternative, whereas middle-class children prefer the second. Perhaps the lower-class child develops little capacity to "delay gratification" because, for him, the future is uncertain and he is frequently frustrated in attempting to satisfy his basic needs. Since he cannot depend on future gratifications, he acts in accordance with the philosophy that "a bird in the hand is worth two in the bush."

Lower-class adults tend to think of personal relationships in terms of power. They have very little voice in decisions that affect their daily lives, and in their work they are usually directed and supervised by others. Advancement in rank or wages is more likely to be due to group efforts (for example, unions) than to individual initiative. In contrast, the work of the middle-class adult is more likely to involve some policy making, self-direction, and autonomy; success in work is more likely to be the result of his own initiative and skill. These social-class differences in life style and philosophy are reflected in techniques of child rearing and training. Thus, the power orientation of the lower-class parent is seen in his frequent use of direct commands, threats, deprivation, and coercive punishment. The middle-class parent, more concerned with feelings and interpersonal relations, is more likely to use love-oriented discipline (withdrawal of affection, disapproval, shame, guilt) in dealing with his child.

As would be expected, middle-class parents stress achievement motivation, learning, and educational accomplishment much more than lower-class parents. In one study, black mothers from four different social classes were asked to teach their four-year-old children several tasks that they themselves had been taught by the investigator.

> Middle-class mothers were more likely to provide an orientation to the task for the child, to request verbal feedback rather than physical compliance, to be specific in their instructions, to use motivation techniques that involved explicit or implicit reward, and, on a number of

measures, to provide the child with information he needed to complete the task and to monitor his performance.

These studies of observed maternal behavior agree in their portrayal of middle-class mothers as more attentive and more responsive to their children, and apparently more aware of their children's feelings and perspectives on the activities in which they are engaged. . . . They also tend less to use power-oriented punishment in influence techniques, are more likely to explain to the child the rationale involved in a request and to provide ideas and words through which maternal control can be mediated.*

Training for independence and self-reliance begins earlier in the middle class than in the lower class. As a consequence, middle-class pre-adolescent and adolescent boys show stronger achievement motivation, as measured by personality tests, interviews about job aspirations, and teacher ratings.

Ethnic groups within a society such as ours also differ markedly in their emphasis on achievement motivation. A large number of mothers and sons from six American ethnic groups—French Canadians, southern Italians, Greeks, Eastern European Jews, northeastern U.S. blacks, and native-born white Protestants—were interviewed about independence training, orientations toward achievement, and vocational and occupational aspirations. Jewish mothers expressed the highest aspirations for their sons and expected them to be independent and self-reliant at a relatively early age. These mothers, as well as Greek, white Protestant, and black mothers, encouraged active, future-oriented, individualistic values and had higher educational and occupational aspirations for their sons than did southern Italian and French-Canadian mothers. Although black mothers also expressed individualistic goals and high educational aspirations for their sons, they had, probably realistically, the lowest occupational goals of all the groups. As would be predicted from their mothers' attitudes and aspirations, the Jewish, Greek, and white Protestant boys had higher achievement motivation than did Italians, French Canadians, and blacks.

* R. D. Hess, "Class and Ethnic Influences upon Socialization," in *Carmichael's Manual of Child Psychology*, 3rd ed. (New York: Wiley, 1970), 2:480.

Personality Development

II: FAMILIAL, PEER, AND
SITUATIONAL INFLUENCES

chapter five

As our discussion in Chapter Four made clear, socialization is strongly influenced by *cultural prescriptions*. However, these prescriptions must be initially communicated to the child by members of his family, the representatives of the culture with whom he has the most intimate relationships.

A child's first social learning occurs at home; his earliest experiences with his family—particularly the bond with his mother—are generally assumed to be critical antecedents of his later social relationships.

Typically, the mother gratifies the infant's primary needs for food, for alleviation of pain, for warmth, and perhaps even for tactile stimulation (which may be a basic, innate drive). Consequently, the mother's presence—the visual, auditory, tactile, and kinesthetic stimuli she presents—becomes associated with the satisfaction of needs, and she begins to stand for pleasure, relief of tension, and contentment.

The earliest meaningful mother-child relationship has generally been referred to as *attachment*, or sometimes *dependency*, which is actually a reciprocal relationship. "The helpless infant elicits caretaking and other responses from the mother and the mother in turn evokes visual regard, vocalization, smiles and approach movements from the infant. These infant responses in turn stimulate further nurturant and affectionate behavior in the mother."*

Attachment can develop only after the infant has acquired certain perceptual and cognitive abilities. He must be able to establish boundaries between himself and the external world, discriminate between people and inanimate objects, and recognize his mother. During the first few months, the infant is indiscriminate in his social responsiveness. But he very soon begins to differentiate between his mother and others, smiling and vocalizing more and more vigorously toward her than toward others, fixating her visually for longer periods of time, and readily allowing himself to be soothed by her. As he forms an elaborate and coherent concept of his mother, he begins to develop certain expectations of her. He searches for her and approaches her whenever he is hungry, in pain, uncomfortable, or afraid. If the mother is nurturant and gratifies his needs promptly and effectively, she rewards the child's "approach responses" to her, and these are likely to be repeated.

Attachment cannot be measured directly. In most studies, it is inferred from the infant's fear of strangers (*stranger anxiety*) and from *separation protest* (crying and fussing when the mother leaves). It is assumed that the child's fear of strangers demonstrates that he discriminates strangers from his mother, and separation protest indicates that he has established a strong, positive relationship with the mother. By five months of age, many infants show stranger anxiety—frowning, crying, and withdrawing from anyone unfamiliar—and the response is most common among infants approximately eight months of age. Separation protest (measured by intensity of the infant's reaction to situations like being left alone in a dark room or being left in a crib at night) reaches its peak at about ten months of age and then declines.

One of the most important antecedents of attachment is maternal sensitivity and responsiveness to the infant's needs and signals. Infants showing strong attachments have mothers who notice their babies' needs and signals, interpret them accurately, and respond to them promptly and appropriately. The mothers of infants with weak attachments ignore them for long periods or misinterpret their signals. Frequent and varied social stimulation by the mother also predisposes the infant to forming strong attachments. Mothers who are demonstrative, engage their babies' attention frequently, and interact with them over long periods of time promote attachment and dependency. In short, the basic requirements for close mother-child relationships are maternal warmth, nurturance, and interest in the baby.

* L. J. Yarrow and F. A. Pedersen, "Attachment: Its Origins and Course," in *The Young Child: Reviews of Research*, ed. W. W. Hartup (Washington, D.C.: National Association for the Education of Young Children, 1972) 2:54.

FIGURE 5.1. From W. Kennedy, *Child Psychology* (Englewood Cliffs, N.J.: Prentice-Hall, Inc., 1972). Photo by John Okladek.

According to many theorists and clinicians, the development of attachment—and the interdependence and intense feeling involved—is the foundation of a *sense of trust* in others and in the world. If the mother is the source of rewarding, gratifying experiences, the infant will trust her. This trust will generalize to others, and will be reflected in favorable social attitudes and friendly, outgoing approaches to other people. In contrast, a mother who is not dependable, and does not minister to the infant's needs promptly or adequately, does not evoke attachment from her child. Rather, her neglect produces a sense of distrust in the child, which he also generalizes to others.

Erik Erikson, a well-known Harvard University psychoanalyst, states that

> experiences connected with feeding are a prime source for the development of trust. At around four months of age a hungry baby will grow quiet and show signs of pleasure at the sound of an approaching footstep, anticipating (trusting) that he will be held and fed. This repeated experience of being hungry, seeing food, receiving food, and feeling relieved and comforted assures the baby that the world is a dependable place.*

Other developmental psychologists agree with Erikson's ideas:

> The development of specific expectations towards the mother is followed by the emergence of a higher level of relationship, the development of confidence or trust. The infant shows this trust by being able to wait if expected gratifications are not immediately forthcoming. He has the confident expectation that his mother will respond to him in predictable ways, that she will soothe him, or provide the objects necessary for his gratification. This trust is associated with strong affective involvement and mutual interdependence. At a later age, he evidences confidence in leaving the mother and exploring a strange environment, secure in the knowledge that his mother will be there to comfort him. Although the quality of attachment changes throughout the developmental cycle, trust and positive emotional involvement remain the core elements.†

These writings clearly imply that strong attachments to the mother during infancy have positive effects on the infant's subsequent development and adjustment. Indeed, there is substantial evidence that supports this view. Infants reared in emotionally cold and unstimulating environments—for example, in institutions where the care is routine and there is very little individual attention—do not readily form attachments to others. Pediatricians have noted that infants reared in such settings tend to be quiet, passive, inactive, unhappy, and emotionally disturbed.

* The Course of Healthy Personality Development" (Midcentury White House Conference on Children and Youth), in *The Adolescent: A Book of Readings*, ed. J. M. Seidman (New York: Holt, Rinehart and Winston, 1960), p. 219.
† Yarrow and Pedersen, "Attachment," p. 59.

Systematic studies reinforce these clinical findings, showing that early attachment to the mother—or to a mother substitute (surrogate)—generally benefits the infant, while failure to develop such attachments has immediate and enduring adverse consequences.

A fascinating series of experimental animal studies conducted by Harry Harlow of the University of Wisconsin is highly relevant to this issue. In one study, two wire "surrogate mothers" were set up in a cubicle attached to a newborn monkey's cage. One surrogate had a bare body of welded wire while the other was covered with soft terrycloth. For some newborn monkeys the cloth mothers gave milk and the wire mothers did not; for other monkey infants this condition was reversed.

The terrycloth mother thus supplied both food and considerable tactile stimulation for some monkeys, while the wire mother gave food but not the same tactile stimulation. When the baby monkeys could go to either mother, they characteristically chose the terrycloth one and spent more time clinging to her, thus giving evidence of attachment. Even those fed by the wire mother showed "attachment" to the terrycloth one. When a frightening wooden spider suddenly appeared in his cage, a young monkey would usually run to the terrycloth mother, the more effective source of security.

> The initial haven was a cloth surrogate for about 70 percent of the one-month-old monkeys and 80 percent of the two-month-old monkeys. Many of the responses to wire surrogates were momentary and were quickly reversed, as if the terror-stricken baby had dashed blindly to any object in the immediacy of need, and finding the wire surrogate comfortless, quickly reversed its choice and sought the security of any cloth surrogate, lactating or non-lactating.*

Harlow concluded that the comfort of tactile stimulation is innately security-giving to the infant animal, so he forms a strong attachment to whatever or whomever offers it.

Studies of human infants are, of course, more directly relevant to students of developmental psychology. In one study, the subjects were infant orphans who had been reared in a deprived, psychologically inadequate institution during the first few months of their lives. Some of them were moved to a much more stimulating setting where each was cared for in an individualized way by one young woman, talked to, played with, and given toys. These children improved markedly in mental alertness and in intelligence; the average gain in intelligence test score was 27 points. A control group of children, who remained in

* H. F. Harlow, *Learning to Love* (San Francisco: Albion Publishing Co., 1971), p. 26.

FIGURE 5.2   When frightened or in need of comfort, infant monkeys seek out the terrycloth mother even if the wire mesh mother "feeds" them. (Courtesy of Prof. Harry Harlow)

the unstimulating institution, showed an average decline of 16 points during the same period.

Other consequences of emotionally inadequate rearing of infants were demonstrated in a study conducted in Iran. Infants in a deprived orphanage—where they were handled impersonally, had no toys, and had little opportunity to practice motor activities—were compared with a group in an enriched orphanage where they received more personal attention, had more toys, and enjoyed greater opportunities for motor practice. The children in the enriched orphanage were considerably more content, emotionally more mature, and happier than the others, and during their second year they were more advanced in motor ability.

It is possible to do interesting experimental work and to be very humane at the same time, as the following relevant study shows. A kindly woman psychologist became the "mother" of eight babies in an orphange for eight weeks. She established a warm, intimate relationship with each of her charges, attended to their needs personally for eight hours a day, played with them, smiled, cooed, and talked to them. A control group of eight infants were handled in a routine, impersonal, though kindly way by various members of the staff of the institution. These latter infants had little individualized attention and formed no attachments to adults.

The two groups of infants showed pronounced behavioral differences by the end of the experimental period. Those who had become attached to their mother surrogate were friendly and outgoing, vocalizing, cooing, and smiling when the experimenter-mother or strangers smiled at them or talked to them. The controls were much less sociable and gave much less evidence of being interested in others.

LONG-TERM EFFECTS OF EARLY MATERNAL TREATMENT

Failure to develop strong attachment to the mother early in infancy may also have very important adverse long-term effects. Harlow kept some monkey infants of both sexes in individual wire cages so that they had no contacts with mothers during the early months of their lives; obviously, they were deprived of maternal attachment and affection. As adults each of these socially deprived monkeys was paired with a normal monkey of the opposite sex. The deprived animals were unable to establish affectional relations or engage in normal sexual activity. For example, deprived males displayed too much aggression, made threatening gestures, and even physically attacked their female partners. Deprived females would permit normal males to come close for very brief periods of time —responding to the male initiative—but avoided being near the males for more than a minute at a time. "Evidently the failure to experience affection early in life rules out the possibility of later reproductive heterosexual relations."*

Without direct evidence, we cannot generalize from these conclusions about the effects of early affectional deprivation on sexual behavior. However, there is abundant evidence that early institutionalization and the consequent failure to form attachments may lead to subsequent cognitive deficiencies and personality maladjustments. One investigator compared two groups of orphans reared in different settings during their first three years. The children in one group had been adopted into foster homes as young infants and had had an opportunity to form attachments to their foster mothers because they had been given individual attention, nurturance, warmth, and adequate mothering. The other group had remained in an institution for three years, receiving impersonal care and inadequate mothering; they had had no intense affectional relationships with any particular mother figure. Many of these latter children were placed in foster homes after three years in the institution.

* Harlow, *Learning to Love*, p. 59.

The researcher studied the children longitudinally at four ages—three-and-a-half, six-and-a-half, eight-and-a-half, and twelve. He observed and interviewed them, and gave them tests of intelligence, educational achievement, personality, motor coordination, social maturity, and language ability.

The institution-reared group were relatively retarded intellectually. At all ages they performed more poorly than the foster-home children on intelligence tests, especially in the areas of concept formation, reasoning, and abstract thinking. Language and speech difficulties were more common among the institution-reared children and persisted long after they left the orphanage.

Personality and adjustment also appeared to be affected adversely by institutional upbringing. Those reared in the orphanage were more maladjusted than the others; they lacked self-control and behaved more aggressively. They were more distractable and hyperactive, and they more frequently lied, stole, destroyed property, threw temper tantrums, and hit and kicked others. In addition, they were more dependent on adults, demanding attention frequently and asking for help unnecessarily.

Institution-reared children had not developed a basic sense of trust in others. Their social relationships were superficial, and they remained emotionally withdrawn and unresponsive, avoiding strong affectionate attachments. The investigator concluded that social and emotional maladjustment persisting into adolescence were the results of the severe deprivations and the emotional unresponsiveness of their early environment.

In interpreting these findings, we must keep in mind that these striking effects were noted among children who were *markedly* deprived of personal, warm, maternal care in the earliest years. The consequences of lesser degrees of deprivation—that is, mildly inadequate mothering, and consequently weaker attachments—are unknown.

CHILD-REARING TECHNIQUES
DURING THE SECOND YEAR

During the child's second year many new and important cognitive, motor, and language skills emerge. The child's understanding of the world increases and his ability to think and solve problems improves; concomitantly, he learns to walk and his manual skills and motor coordination progress rapidly; his language competence increases enormously. The two-year-old enjoys trying out his new skills and abilities, investigating his surroundings, and testing his new capacities. If his parents encourage the child to explore freely, rewarding his curiosity and independent behavior, he is apt to continue to investigate his surroundings and attempt to manipulate the environment actively. Such a child is likely to develop spontaneity, curiosity, and self-confidence, together with strong drives for autonomy, independence, mastery, competence and achievement.

Parents who severely restrict their child's freedom of movement may inhibit his tendencies to explore and to investigate, and thus stifle the development of motivations for autonomy and independence. Some mothers find it difficult to deal with active, running, jumping, climbing children who seem to be into everything; hence, they discourage the child's exploration and his attempts to experiment. Other mothers are overprotective, tending to baby their children, discouraging independence and attempting to keep them close and clinging—perhaps because they regard independence as a threat to their own domination, control, and possession of the children. Many overprotected children become submissive and compliant; unable or afraid to make spontaneous responses; inhibited in investigating, exploring, and experimenting; shy and withdrawn in social situations. These children lack persistence; they give up readily when faced with difficult tasks or problems, probably as a result of lack of rewards for early problem-solving efforts and because of their parents' tendency to solve problems for them. Since persistence is often necessary for learning academic subjects, an overprotected child may be at a disadvantage when he enters school.

Parental stimulation and encouragement of the child's independent achievements, exploration, and attempts at mastery may affect his later behavior in positive ways. For example, among nursery school children, those with mothers who encourage early independence and achievement tend to be more interested than others in mastery and achievement. They spend more time in challenging and creative activities such as painting, making clay models, and reading books. When they reach school age they are, according to personality tests, more highly motivated for achievement, and their grades are better than those of children who were not rewarded for early strivings for independence. Apparently, strong motivation to learn and to perform well in school is fostered by parental encouragement of competence and exploration early in life. Moreover, motivation for achievement appears to be a stable aspect of personality. If it develops early, it is likely to be maintained over a long span of years.

THE EFFECTS OF DIFFERENT TYPES
OF HOME ATMOSPHERES

As the child matures and grows in capability, his relationships with his parents become more complex and subtle. Broad, global features of the home—features such as warmth, democracy, intellectuality, affectionateness, friction, permissiveness (or restrictiveness), punitiveness, firmness of discipline—begin to have more impact on the child.

A classic investigation of the relationship between these kinds of variables and children's behavior was conducted at the Fels Institute in Yellow Springs, Ohio. A home visitor—a highly trained, perceptive woman—visited the homes of the nursery school subjects and observed the interactions among family members. Then she rated each home on thirty carefully defined qualities that together provided an objective, well-rounded description of the home atmosphere. The children's personality characteristics were rated independently on the basis of systematic observations of their behavior in school.

Democratic homes were those characterized by parental encouragement of the child's curiosity and self-expression, frequent discussions between parent and child, and consultations about decisions. Most democratic homes were also judged to be high in warmth, and provided strong emotional support for the child. Children from these homes were rated high in leadership, activity, outgoingness, assertiveness, creativity, originality, constructiveness, curiosity, nonconformity, and disobedience. In brief, they were highly energetic, socially active children, relatively uninhibited in expressing feelings and emotions, including protests against authorities, such as teachers. Apparently behaviors encouraged and rewarded in democratic homes—curiosity, exploration, experimentation, active attempts to cope with new problems, expression of feelings and ideas—generalize to the nursery school. In contrast, children brought up in homes rated high in *control*—characterized by many clearcut rules, prohibitions, and restrictions—tended to be quiet, well behaved, shy, socially unassertive, inhibited, highly conforming, and lacking in curiosity and creativity. In these homes, children were rewarded for conforming behavior and they were discouraged from exploration, independent activities, and experimentation. These responses learned at home also generalize; in nursery school these children appear conforming, timid, awkward, and apprehensive.

A series of studies completed within the last few years at the University of California at Berkeley focused on the kinds of parent-child relationships related to competence, self-reliance, and independence in young children. Nursery school children were intensively observed and rated in terms of self-control, curiosity about new and exciting stimuli, self-reliance, and general mood (impression of pleasure and enthusiasm). Three contrasting groups of children were delineated: first, the most self-reliant, self-controlled, explorative, and contented children; second, discontented, withdrawn, and distrustful children; and third, the least self-reliant, explorative, and self-controlled. Visits to the children's homes and structured observations of interactions between parents and children provided the major data used to rate aspects of child rearing—specifically, maternal *control, maturity demands* (pressures on the child to perform at the level of his ability and to make decisions on his own), *clarity of communication,* and *parental nurturance* (warmth toward the child and involvement with him).

The results showed that the three groups of children experienced vastly different patterns of child rearing. For example, parents of children in the first group (the most mature, competent, and self-reliant) were rated high in all four parent-child dimensions; that is, these parents were controlling and demanding but at the same time they were warm, rational, communicative, and receptive to their children's communications. The investigator labeled this pattern *authoritative;* it involves a balance between nurturance and control, high demands and clear communications, together with encouragement of the child's independent exploration.

The parents of the discontented, withdrawn, and distrustful children in the second group were themselves detached and controlling, less warm and more punitive than the parents in the other groups. They were called *authoritarian* parents.

Parents of children in the third group, the least self-reliant and self-controlled, were *permissive* (warm, supportive, and nurturant, but inclined to be overprotective and lax in discipline); they made few demands on their children and did little to encourage independence.

In a further study of these relationships, the investigator refined and elaborated the definitions of the three types of child rearing. She then related these practices to competence, independence, and responsibility in another large group of young boys and girls. Note the contrasts in the following brief summaries of the three parental patterns.

The *authoritarian* parent attempts to shape and control the child's behavior and attitudes according to a set standard of conduct. Important virtues are obedience, respect for authority, respect for work and for order. Punitive, forceful means are used to discipline the child; verbal give-and-take is not encouraged.

The *authoritative* parent, by contrast, attempts to direct the child's activity in a rational way, encouraging verbal communication and informing the child of the reasoning behind her policies. She values her child's self-expression, independence, individual interests, and unique characteristics. Hence, although she exerts firm control at times, she does not hem in the child with restrictions.

The *permissive* parent is nonpunitive, accepting the child's impulses, desires, and actions. She makes few demands on the child for responsibility or for order, allowing him to regulate his own activities as much as possible. She avoids controlling the child, consults with him about policy decisions, and gives explanations for family rules.*

* Descriptions of parents summarized from D. Baumrind, "Authoritarian vs. Authoritative Parent Control," *Adolescence* 3 (1968):255–72.

The study showed clearly that *authoritative* parents most effectively promote the development of competence, responsibility, and independence. High demands for maturity and firmness in disciplinary matters appear to be associated with both self-assertion and social responsibility in young children. Compared with permissive and authoritarian parents, those who are authoritative are more likely to produce responsible, friendly, cooperative, and achievement-oriented children, especially if they are boys. The investigator suggests that although both authoritative and authoritarian parents preach responsible behavior, the latter do not practice it; they are more concerned with their own ideas and standards than with the child's interests and welfare. Authoritative parents, on the other hand, both preach and practice responsible behavior; hence, their children behave more responsibly. Permissive parents do little to encourage or reward responsible behavior or to discourage immature behavior. Their sons are clearly lacking in responsibility and achievement-oriented behavior.

Independence and achievement orientation in girls are clearly associated with authoritative upbringing; in boys, nonconforming parental behavior and, to a lesser extent, authoritative upbringing are associated with these characteristics. The investigator concluded that

> parents who provided the most enriched environment, namely the nonconforming and the authoritative parents, had the most dominant and purposive children. These parents, by comparison with the others studied, set high standards of excellence, invoked cognitive insight, provided an intellectually stimulating atmosphere, were themselves rated as being differentiated and individualistic, and made high educational demands upon the child.*

Although the two parent-child studies discussed above were conducted in different places and at different times, using different research techniques, there are several important themes running throughout the findings. Warmth, support, and nurturance from the parents are critical antecedents of children's maturity, independence, self-reliance, competence, and responsibility. But love and support are not enough to assure the development of these characteristics. Other prerequisites are adequate communication between parents and children; the use of reason rather than punishment in achieving compliance; parental respect for the child's autonomy; encouragement of independence, individuality, and responsibility; and relatively firm control and high demands for mature behavior.

---

* D. Baumrind, "Socialization and Instrumental Competence in Young Children," in *The Young Child: Reviews of Research*, ed. W. W. Hartup (Washington, D.C.: National Association for the Education of Young Children, 1972) 2:217.

In short, authoritative interactions—but not blind, authoritarian discipline—facilitate the development of mature personal and social behavior.

IDENTIFICATION

As we have seen, many of the child's response patterns, characteristics, attitudes, and motives are acquired as a result of social learning and rewards at home. Other complicated reactions, behavior patterns, and motivational and emotional tendencies appear to be acquired spontaneously without direct training and without specific rewards. You have no doubt observed four-year-old girls whose posture, ways of moving, gestures, and speech inflections are duplicates of their mothers'. It is not likely that their mothers consciously "taught" their daughters to emulate them in these ways; nor is it likely that they rewarded them directly for imitating their behaviors and mannerisms. In short, the mothers did not intend to teach these responses and the children did not intend to learn them. A more subtle process, *identification*, is involved.

Identification may be regarded as a *learned drive or motive to be like another individual*. When a child identifies with someone else, he thinks, behaves, and feels as though the other person's characteristics were his own. The child is identifying with a parent when he attempts to duplicate in his own life the ideals, attitudes, and behavior of that parent. The person or group with whom the child identifies is referred to as the *model* or *identificand*.

Identification is a fundamental mechanism of personality development and socialization. By identifying with his parents, a child acquires many of their ways of behaving, thinking, and feeling. Moreover, since the parents are representatives of their culture, the child's identification with them provides him with skills, temperamental qualities, attitudes, motives, ideals, values, taboos, and morals appropriate for his cultural group. Through identification, as well as through learning by reward, the American middle-class child becomes competitive and achievement-oriented; the Hopi child becomes cooperative and democratic; Mundugamor boys in New Guinea become harsh and aggressive; Japanese children become passive, accepting, and group-oriented.

Furthermore, through parental identification, the child incorporates his culture's moral standards, values, and judgments, the components of what Freud calls the *superego*. Then he punishes himself, largely by feeling guilty or anxious, whenever he does—or is tempted to do—something that is prohibited or immoral.

In addition, the child's identification with the parent of his or her own sex leads to appropriate sex typing—the boy's adoption of patterns of behavior that will be appropriate to his role as a man in his culture, the girl's incorporation of characteristics that characterize females in her culture. The definitions of male and female behavior vary from culture to culture, and they may change considerably over time within a complex culture. Sex differences in aggression, submissiveness, dependency, and achievement orientation are primarily shaped by cultural prescription and hence can be modified. Sex-typed characteristics are not inherent in the biological structures of the two sexes; they are not innate or immutable. There is no biological basis for many of the standard or stereotyped patterns of "masculine" and "feminine" characteristics, no *biological* reason for females to be passive, dependent, and noncompetitive, or to play down their intellectual potential and devote themselves exclusively to home and family. In our American society there are substantial *cultural* pressures to become feminine in stereotyped ways; yet many women are independent, self-assertive, and achievement-oriented—and it appears that in the near future there will be many more. If these women have daughters who identify with them, these girls will also adopt these characteristics.

Identification begins early in life, and is a prolonged—perhaps lifelong —process. As a child matures, he continues to identify with his parents, acquiring more of their characteristics. As his social world expands, however, he finds other identification models among his peers, teachers, ministers, and heroes from fiction, movies, and TV, and he emulates their behavior, characteristics, and ideals. In the end, the individual's personality will be based on a long series of identifications; he will have incorporated some of his parents' characteristics, but he will also have adopted the behavior and ideas of a number of others. Since his personality is in large part derived from many different identifications, it will be complex and unique.

Erikson suggests that adolescence is a critical period for the integration and synthesis of past identifications, for dropping some and strengthening others. The adolescent faces an *identity crisis* that involves "finding himself" and arriving at some satisfactory answer to the question, "Who am I?"

> The identity the adolescent seeks to clarify is who he is, what his role in society is to be: Is he a child or is he an adult? Does he have it in him to be someday a husband and father? What is he to be as a worker and an earner of money? Can he feel self-confident in spite of the fact that his race or religious or national background makes him a person some people look down upon? Overall, will he be a success or a failure? By reason of these questions adolescents are sometimes morbidly preoccupied with how they appear in the eyes of others as compared with their own conception of themselves. . . .*

* "Healthy Personality Development," p. 215.

Earlier identifications and past learning and experience provide a foundation for a new and unique sense of *ego identity*, but "the whole has a different quality than the sum of the parts."* If he achieves a substantial sense of ego identity, the adolescent begins to regard himself as an individual—a self-consistent, integrated, unique person, worthy of the recognition of others. He is comfortable with himself, knows where he is going, and is not overly self-conscious or self-doubting. Failure to acquire a coherent sense of ego identity is called *ego diffusion*—the individual has not "found himself," is uncertain of his value as an individual, and lacks a sense of purpose in life.

Research on identification.   How is an identification with a model formed, and what are the underlying motivations? One hypothesis, based on social-learning theory, maintains that the motivation to identify with a model is rooted in the satisfactions derived from interactions with that model. A model who gratifies a child's needs becomes associated with feelings of satisfaction, pleasure, and comfort. He as a person, his behavior, and his characteristics—all acquire reward value for the child. By identifying with this model, and thus incorporating his characteristics and behavior, the child becomes the source of his own rewards; he can now react to himself with the feelings of gratification that were originally associated with the model.

Support for this general hypothesis has been found in a number of investigations. In one study, two groups of mother-daughter pairs were the subjects. One group of mothers were judged to be nurturant (warm, giving, attentive, gratifying to the child), while the other group of mothers were judged not to be. Each mother was observed as she was teaching her daughter, a kindergarten pupil, to solve some maze problems. During the teaching session, each mother—the model in this situation—acting on instructions from the experimenter, added a number of extraneous actions that had nothing to do with solving the problem. For example, she may have drawn her lines very slowly, hesitated briefly at each choice point, made some unnecessary marks such as circles or loops in her tracing, and made some meaningless comments before each trial. The daughters of the nurturant mothers imitated many of these irrelevant, incidental behaviors, but the daughters of the nonnurturant mothers imitated very few. Thus, as the hypothesis predicted, mothers who were warm and gratifying elicited greater identification from their daughters —and more emulation of their behavior—than mothers who lacked these qualities.

* Erik Erikson, "Identity and the Life Cycle," *Psychological Issues* 1 (1959): 90.

Nursery school boys and their families were the subjects of another study. Parental child-rearing practices were evaluated by interviews with the parents, and each child was observed during projective doll play—a procedure in which the child was told to "make up a story" using toy furniture and a set of dolls representing a mother, father, and siblings. The content of the play was examined to determine which family doll the child identified with most commonly, that is, the role he took in acting out his story. The sons of warm, permissive, easygoing fathers frequently played the father's role—an indication of their identification with the father—but sons of fathers lacking these characteristics seldom played this role in their stories.

Experimental studies of imitation. Several ingenious experimental studies of the imitation of models also confirm the above findings. In one, nursery school boys and girls had different kinds of experiences with an adult model who was a confederate of the experimenter. The model first met with each child in a playroom setting. With half the children she acted warm, affectionate, and nurturant; she was much less responsive and more distant in her interactions with the other children.

Immediately following the first interaction, the model took each child to an experimental room "to play a special game with a toy cash register." As she played the game with the child, she did many neutral things that were unrelated to the "game" (for example, she marched around the room and uttered some sounds and words). Also, some of her reactions were distinctly aversive or punitive to the subject (criticizing him and delaying rewards).

At the end of this session, the child was left alone to play with the cash register for three minutes, and during this time his behavior was observed through a one-way screen. Next, the child was taken back to the playroom and told that as a special treat he was going to be allowed to show someone else—a girl dressed as a clown—how to play the cash register game. The measure of the imitation of the model's behavior was the number of times the subject copied the model's irrelevant or aversive behaviors in the presence of the model, during the interval when he was alone in the experimental room, and during the time he spent with the clown.

The nurtured, rewarded group imitated more of the model's neutral behaviors than did the other group in all three situations. Even more impressively, the nurtured group imitated more of the model's *aversive* behaviors in their interactions with the other child after the experimental session. Apparently, all of the model's responses, neutral and aversive, are more likely to be imitated if he or she is initially warm, affectionate, and nurturant.

CONSCIENCE DEVELOPMENT

Since superego or conscience development is one of the major products of identification, we might expect morality in children to be related to identification and, therefore, to positive relationships with parents. And, indeed, there is evidence that this is the case, although it is extremely difficult to assess conscience development. One technique involves determining children's reactions to their own transgressions or wrongdoing. What does the child do if he breaks something, hits someone, or takes something without permission? Does he feel guilty, confess, apologize, try to make restitution? Or does he lie, hide, and deny the wrongdoing?

The basic data of one study were mothers' reports of both parent-child relations and their children's reactions to their own transgressions. Analysis of the data showed that warm mothers tended to produce children who confessed their deviations, indicating guilt and strong conscience development. Boys who had accepting fathers also showed more guilt following wrongdoing and higher levels of conscience development than boys with rejecting fathers.

A high degree of conscience is promoted by the use of love-oriented disciplinary techniques, that is, techniques in which love is given or withheld to reward or to punish the child. Praise and reasoning as disciplinary techniques are associated with high conscience in children, whereas physical punishment is related to poor conscience development. The use of love-oriented disciplinary techniques is only effective for warm and loving mothers who maintain strong and affectionate relationships with their children. Children are in fact most likely to develop a high level of conscience if they have affectionate mothers who threaten to withdraw love as punishment for disobedience. Conscience appears to be a consequence of an identification based on the child's fear of loss of love of an otherwise warm and loving parent.

> Withdrawing love where little exists is meaningless. If the mother is relatively cold to begin with, then using withdrawal of love should have little effect on conscience development. The pattern most calculated to produce "high conscience" should be that of mothers who are usually warm and loving and then, as a method of control, threaten this affectionate relationship.
>
> ... This is indeed the case. The children most prone to behave in ... ways ... indicative of having a well-developed conscience were those whose mothers were relatively warm toward them but who made their love contingent on the child's good behavior. These were the children who truly were risking the loss of love when they misbehaved.*

* R. R. Sears, E. E. Maccoby, and H. Levin, *Patterns of Child Rearing* (New York: Harper & Row, 1957), pp. 388–89.

Generosity, another aspect of moral behavior, is also related to identification. In one study, nursery school boys participated in a simple experiment, were rewarded with a number of trinkets for their participation, and were then given an opportunity to share their "winnings" with other children. Those who shared generously and those who did not were then observed in doll-play situations. The generous boys portrayed their fathers in doll play as warm, giving, nurturant, and affectionate, but these kinds of father-perceptions were significantly less frequent among boys who were not generous.

Juvenile delinquency may be regarded as a manifestation of deficient conscience development, a failure to incorporate or accept some of the culture's moral and ethical standards and prohibitions. This is a very complex problem; many factors are salient antecedents of delinquent behavior. Social and economic factors obviously play a major part, for delinquency rates are highest among the very poor and among disadvantaged minority and immigrant groups. These factors are not sufficient to produce delinquency, however; many children who grow up in poverty or have immigrant or minority parents do not become delinquent.

Studies conducted in different geographic areas and with different socioeconomic groups consistently show that delinquent behavior is related to failure to identify with parents and, consequently, to incorporate the culture's moral and ethical standards. Parents of delinquents, compared with those of nondelinquents of comparable intelligence and social status, are generally less affectionate, more indifferent, and more hostile toward them, and show less warmth and sympathy. Relatively few delinquents have close ties to their fathers, and many of them express open hostility toward both parents.

Peers as Agents of Socialization

During the first few years, the child's social interactions are restricted largely to his own family circle, and his models for identification are parents and siblings. When he enters nursery school, the child's social world expands and increases in complexity and intensity. Peers become influential agents of socialization, "training" by reinforcing certain responses and serving as models for imitation and identification. As a result, the young child's behavior, attitudes, and motivations may undergo major changes, although not all children are equally affected by contacts with peers. Those who are shy and withdrawn are less likely to have intensive interactions with other children and are therefore less likely to be influenced by them. Outgoing, explorative, relatively independent children are more likely to participate in social activities and are consequently more susceptible to influence. Popular nursery school children have a broader range of social contacts, give others more rewards, and are more often the targets of rewards; they are more likely to influence their peers and in turn be influenced by them.

From an adult point of view, some of the changes in the child's behavior are desirable, others undesirable. Kindness, cooperation, and friendliness are likely to bring rewards from peers and hence are likely to be repeated and strengthened. Some behaviors bring peer disapproval and punishment—selfishness, dependency, and babyishness, for example —and these responses are likely to be weakened or eliminated (extinguished).

Aggressive behavior is often rewarded in nursery school and is thus likely to be strengthened. If a child is already highly aggressive when he begins nursery school, he is likely to become even more aggressive because other children reward this behavior by yielding to his wishes, withdrawing from conflict, and permitting him to obtain what he wants. Children who are relatively unaggressive initially are also likely to become more aggressive. While they may be frequent targets of aggression at first, many such children eventually counterattack and refuse to give up things they want to keep. Their new assertive and aggressive reactions are likely to be successful and hence to become stronger and more frequent. Some children are initially unaggressive and at the same time very passive and socially withdrawn; these children are not likely to counterattack when they are the targets of aggression, and hence are not rewarded for aggressive behavior. These are the only children who are not likely to become more aggressive in nursery school.

PEERS AS MODELS

Nursery school children readily identify with other children and spontaneously imitate the model's behavior, both desirable and undesirable. Those who are at first mild-mannered are likely to become more assertive if they observe their playmates using force and threats to attain goals. A child will readily imitate the aggressive patterns of other children— striking objects, screaming, kicking, destroying things. If he observes these repeatedly, he may adopt them—especially if they are successful in obtaining goals—as his own habitual responses.

Positive social responses (prosocial behavior) may also be modeled and imitated by peers. If kindergarten children play with others who are socially more mature, they themselves become more cooperative, participate in more group activities, and more often use requests and suggestions rather than force in dealing with others. And, as one experiment shows, children's generosity (sharing prizes they win) increases if they observe peer models behaving altruistically. Control subjects, who did not observe generous models, were not nearly as generous in their giving.

As the child grows older and spends more time away from his home and family, his peers become even more influential as teachers and models. During middle childhood, the peer group can be very helpful in training the child to adapt to the broader social world. Peers can help him learn how to interact with larger groups and how to relate to leaders, and they can provide the child with some guidance and assistance in achieving better personal adjustment. New and effective ways of dealing with complex feelings—hostility, dominance, dependence, and independence—may be learned from peers, and it may be very reassuring to the child to discover that others his own age share his problems and conflicts. The peer group is probably more influential in present-day American culture than in most other societies. In traditional China, as well as in rural or small-town America in earlier times, children were much more oriented toward their families and much less concerned with their peer group's attitudes and behavior. On the other hand, in societies such as Israeli kibbutzim (communal settlements) and in the Soviet Union, children are as concerned, or perhaps even more concerned, with peer approval as with their family's reactions.

PEER-GROUP INFLUENCES DURING
ADOLESCENCE

For many reasons, peer influences appear to be greatest during adolescence. The adolescent is a marginal person—no longer a child, not yet an adult—and there are many pressures on him. Within a relatively short period of time he must make numerous adjustments. He must gradually achieve independence from his family; adjust to sexual maturity; establish cooperative, workable relationships with peers; decide on and prepare for a vocation; develop some kind of philosophy of life or a set of guiding moral beliefs and standards; and develop a sense of identity. At the same time, ties to parents become progressively weaker as independence is achieved.

Under the circumstances, it is not difficult to understand why the adolescent is likely to feel close to others who have the same problems, who can help him gain clearer concepts of himself, his problems, and his goals. Peers may be more successful than parents in giving the adolescent a feeling of personal worth and realistic perspectives and hopes for the future. The culture has changed extremely rapidly, and in many ways, since the parents of today's adolescents were themselves adolescents. There are new and different pressures to adjust to. Furthermore, watching their adolescent children trying to cope with their problems, parents may find their own adolescent feelings and conflicts reawakened, and this may be extremely uncomfortable. For these reasons, parents often have great difficulties in communicating with their adolescent children and in understanding and sharing their problems, even though they make sincere efforts to do so. Understandably, they worry about the "generation gap."

All of these factors heighten the significance of peer groups during adolescence, and therefore there is strong motivation to conform to the peer-culture values, customs, and fads during this period. Yet it would be a mistake to infer that conformity to peer-group standards inevitably implies diminished parental influence, at least for most adolescents. For one thing, there is usually considerable overlap between parental and peer values because the child's friends are likely to come from the same background. The friends of a white Protestant middle-class adolescent are likely to come from that same group. Furthermore,

> neither parental nor peer influence is monolithic. The weight given to either [parent or peer opinion] will depend to a significant degree on the adolescent's appraisal of its relative value in a specific situation. For example, peer influence is more likely to be predominant in such matters as tastes in music and entertainment, fashions in clothing and language, patterns of same- and opposite-sex peer interaction, and the like; while parental influence is more likely to be predominant in such areas as underlying moral and social values and understanding of the adult world.*

Adolescents are most likely to become very strongly identified with their peer group if their parents fail to provide adequate nurturance and support, that is, if they do not foster strong parental identification. Parental influence is more powerful than peer influence among adolescents whose parents express affection, interest, understanding, and willingness to be helpful. In contrast, according to the data of one study, strongly peer-oriented adolescents rate their parents low in affection, support, and control. In brief,

> the peer-oriented child is more a product of parental disregard than of the attractiveness of the peer group— . . . he turns to his age-mates less by choice than by default. The vacuum left by the withdrawal of parents and adults from the lives of children is filled with . . . the substitute of an age-segregated peer group.†

After an exhaustive review of the relevant literature, one authority on adolescent adjustment concluded that a marked decline in parental influence, accompanied by increase in peer influence, is most likely to occur where

---

* J. J. Conger, "A World They Never Knew: The Family and Social Change," *Daedalus* 100, no. 4 (1971):1128, 1129.

† Ibid., p. 1129.

(1) there is a very strong, homogeneous peer group with patterns of behavior and attitudes that differ markedly from those of parents; (2) a rewarding parent-child relationship is lacking at the outset, due to a lack of parental interest and understanding, manifest willingness to be helpful, and shared family activities; (3) the parents' own values and behaviors are inconsistent, uninformed, unrealistic, maladaptive, or obviously hypocritical; (4) the adolescent lacks either the self-confidence (based on a positive self-image) or the independence training to act autonomously without undue concern; or (5) as it is phrased on multiple-choice examinations, "all of the above." In most cases where young people have forsaken or renounced family values for those of deviant peer groups, one or more of these conditions is likely to obtain.*

Stability of Personality Characteristics

There would be little interest in investigating the antecedents of children's personality characteristics if these characteristics were ephemeral, transient, or highly subject to change. The question of stability or continuity of early-established personality traits is a critical one. If we know what the child is like at four, for example, can we predict accurately what he will be like in the future—at age eight, at adolescence, or in adulthood?

The answer is a qualified affirmative. Many personality characteristics established early in life appear to be stable and enduring; if we know the child's status with respect to certain dimensions of personality—such as introversion, aggression, dependency, general adjustment—we can predict his later standing in these dimensions reasonably well. Adult maladjustment, for example, is often an extension of early-established maladjustments; most emotionally disturbed adults suffered intense conflicts, feelings of rejection, and inadequacy during childhood.

Longitudinal studies offer unique opportunities to investigate the persistence of personality characteristics from childhood to adulthood in normal (nonclinical) populations. A number of these studies show that the dimension of active extroversion—or its opposite, passive introversion—is established very early in life and tends to remain highly stable.

The stability of a number of personality characteristics was investigated in the Fels longitudinal study. The subjects, seventy-one predominantly middle-class people, were studied from birth through early adulthood. Their parents were interviewed and the subjects themselves frequently tested and observed in their homes, nursery schools, day camps, and schools. Personality characteristics such as dependency,

* Ibid., p. 1130.

passivity, aggression, and achievement motivation were rated at five age periods; 0–3, 3–6, 6–10, 10–14, and young adulthood (20–29). The ratings for the four childhood periods were made by a psychologist who had no knowledge of the adult subjects' personality; another psychologist, working independently and knowing nothing about the subjects' early development, interviewed them in depth when they were adults and then rated them on the same variables.

A substantial number of personality characteristics remained stable from childhood through adolescence and adulthood. Motivation to achieve, especially in intellectual tasks, begins to stabilize in the age period from three to six and becomes increasingly stable between six and ten years. Children who showed interest in mastering intellectual skills during the preschool period were likely to be highly motivated for intellectual achievement during elementary school and during adolescence and adulthood. Children who were inhibited and apprehensive in their relationships with others in early childhood (ages six to ten) became tense adults who were uncomfortable in social situations.

Characteristics that have been traditionally sex-typed also showed stability. For example, boys in our culture are generally more aggressive than girls, while girls are more dependent. Measures of aggression were consistently more stable for boys than for girls. Boys who had temper tantrums and displayed rage in the early years of elementary school became easily angered adolescents and, later, adults who were very prone to be verbally aggressive when frustrated. In contrast, dependency and passivity were more stable for girls than for boys. Girls who were highly dependent on others and reacted passively to frustrations during early childhood became passive adolescents, closely tied to their families, and as young women they relied on others to help them solve their problems. Relatively independent adolescent girls were likely to grow into independent and self-sufficient adults.

While some of this evidence is impressive, we must be cautious not to overgeneralize the findings. For one thing, there is little evidence of stability of many characteristics observed in the *very* early periods of life. The results of one longitudinal study suggest that "emotional adjustment as reflected by happy, calm, and positive behavior during the child's first two years may not be predictive of later overt behavior."* Most of the stable traits discussed above began to stabilize during the period from six to ten years; very few stabilized during the preschool period.

Furthermore, correlations between early and later behavior, though positive and significant, are far from perfect. This means that many

* E. S. Schaefer and N. Bayley, *Maternal Behavior, Child Behavior, and Their Intercorrelations from Infancy Through Adolescence*, Monographs of the Society for Research in Child Development, vol. 28, no. 3 (whole no. 87) (1963), p. 48.

people *do* change in characteristics such as achievement motivation, aggression, and dependency, although, for the population at large, they are well formed in early childhood and persist through later periods. But there is little reason to believe that personality development ends in early childhood; rather, it seems clear that many important aspects of personality remain open to change over long spans of time.

Situational Determinants of Behavior

Situational factors—stimuli in the immediately present environment, especially social ones—also exert powerful influences on behavior, and sometimes they are the prepotent determinants of our actions. Whatever their personality structure, Americans drive on the right-hand side of the road, except under very unusual conditions. Whether we are dependent or independent, assertive or unassertive, introverted or extroverted, we do not laugh during religious services, funeral orations, or recitations of marriage vows. The cultural rules for behavior in these settings are set and inflexible; hardly anyone deviates from the standard, culturally prescribed behavior.

For the vast majority of situations that the individual encounters, the rules for behavior are not so rigid, however. In most situations, the child's behavior is a function of *both* his personality characteristics and the immediate environmental conditions. To illustrate, let us look at behavior in a crisis. If a child is basically secure and calm, his behavior ordinarily reflects these characteristics. But faced with an event such as fire, storm, or injury he may display fear or panic. Children who are generally anxious, fearful, and excitable may react even more strongly. To cite a less extreme example, a youngster may be anxious, dependent, and aggressive when he is with his tense and punitive parents, but he may be calm and independent in a relaxed and friendly nursery school atmosphere.

FRUSTRATION AND AGGRESSION

Everyone occasionally encounters a frustration—an obstacle interfering with the achievement of a desired goal. Frustration may be regarded as a *situational* variable, and reactions to it have been studied extensively, both experimentally and in natural settings. One of the most common reactions is aggression. In nursery school, for example, aggressive conflicts between children increase when the amount of play space is limited and when, consequently, there are more frustrations and interferences.

Children subjected to experimentally produced frustrations are likely to react with aggressive responses, especially if they are in a permissive situation where aggression does not lead to punishment. In one study, preschool boys and girls were observed playing with dolls for two thirty-minute sessions. During the first, they were allowed to play freely. But before the second session, one group of subjects, the *failure* or *frustration group*, worked at extremely difficult tasks that made them feel unsuccessful and frustrated. The *control group* was not experimentally frustrated before the second doll-play session.

In the second session, both groups displayed more aggression than they had during the first play period, probably because the permissive atmosphere permitted such expression. The frustration group, however, showed significantly *greater increases in aggression* than the control group. Apparently, the experience of frustration elicited the subsequent heightened aggressiveness.

In a sense, frustration, like beauty, is in the eye of the beholder. The child's *interpretation* of a frustrating situation, rather than any absolute amount of frustration, is most relevant in determining his reactions; and this interpretation may be affected by situational factors. If a child's toy is broken by another child, the victim will react with greater hostility if he interprets the other's action as intentional rather than accidental. In one experiment, children in the third grade were frustrated by a somewhat older child who was a confederate of the experimenter. The frustrator prevented the subjects from completing some simple block-construction tasks, and thus from earning some money. Following the frustration, some of the children were told that the frustrator was tired and upset, that under other conditions he would have been more co-operative. The remainder of the frustrated children, in control groups, were not given these explanations of the extenuating circumstances. Shortly afterward, each subject met the frustrator in another setting and had an opportunity to interfere with or help him. The group that had been given the interpretation of the frustrator's behavior showed significantly less aggression toward him than the control children. In effect, frustration in the "interpretation" group had been reduced, and consequently aggressive expression was also reduced.

The amount of frustration and the perception or interpretation of the frustration are not the only determinants of the intensity of aggressive reactions. Some children become violently aggressive in response to a relatively minor frustration, while others hardly become aggressive at all under the same frustrating circumstances. Why? Because from past experience, some children acquire higher degrees of "tolerance" for frustration (marked ability to endure frustration without becoming upset). Preschool children who according to tests have developed such tolerance display significantly less aggression than children in the same nursery school who experience the same frustrations but have lower tolerances.

Moreover, children differ in the intensity of their acquired fears of punishment for aggressiveness. Among boys studied at one juvenile correctional institution, those with strong fears of punishment for such behavior were less aggressive than their peers who were relatively unafraid, even though the two groups were in the same situation (the institution) and experienced the same frustrations. Apparently, then, the intensity of a child's aggression is a function not only of the situation—although that is important—but also of the personality structure he has developed.

Effects of observing aggression in others.   Violence has become an increasingly prominent subject of the mass media in recent years. Inevitably, the question arises: Does exposure to violence lead to greater aggression in children? Specifically, is the violence observed in movies and on TV likely to augment a child's aggressive tendencies? There are as yet no clearcut answers to these questions, but several research findings are highly relevant. Typically, in experimental studies, subjects are shown films portraying aggressive interaction; control groups are exposed to films of the same length that have no violent content. Following this, the children are given an opportunity to behave aggressively, and those who were exposed to the aggressive films usually show more aggression than the control groups. This experimental finding has been replicated in many studies. Nevertheless, it is hazardous to generalize from these studies conducted in laboratories and using only brief film sequences.

Quite different results came from a more naturalistic study in which exposure to aggression over a six-week period was systematically studied. The subjects were boys between ten and seventeen years of age, some attending private schools and some living in boys' detention homes. Within each institution, boys were assigned randomly either to a television schedule containing predominantly aggressive programs or to a control treatment which involved predominantly nonaggressive programs. All subjects watched a minimum of six hours of television a week but were permitted to view as much as they wanted, provided they saw only programs from their own list. Measures of aggressiveness were administered before and after the experimental period; in addition, a daily behavior rating of each boy was made by his immediate supervisors.

The differences in television programs viewed had little effect on the aggressiveness of the boys in private schools. However, among those in the detention homes, the boys who saw the aggressive programs actually displayed *less* verbal and physical aggression toward peers and toward authorities than those who saw predominantly nonaggressive programs. These effects were most pronounced among boys who were initially impulsive and aggressive.

These data offer little support for the view that exposure to aggressive content in television leads to an increase in aggressive behavior. Rather, the experimental findings . . . suggest that the observation of aggression on television may help control and modulate the expression of aggressive impulses in some of those children who have strong aggressive tendencies. These findings must be interpreted with considerable caution and clearly cannot be generalized to girls or to younger children. They do, however, point to the need for extending laboratory research to more naturalistic settings.*

The question of the effects on children's aggression of viewing violence on the screen is still an open one.

SITUATIONAL DETERMINANTS OF DEPENDENCY

While the strength of a child's dependency needs is to a large extent a consequence of his early relationships with his family and peers, manifestations of dependency are also strongly influenced by the immediate situation. Infants who are away from their mothers for short periods show intense attachment behavior when they are reunited—clinging to the mother and refusing to be put down, crying whenever she leaves, and showing intense fear when approached by strangers. If a mother temporarily provides less nurturance than usual, she may expect her baby to manifest more dependent behavior than he does ordinarily.

The effects on dependency of "social deprivation"—isolation from social contacts or a reduction in the normal level of social interaction—have been studied extensively. For example, in one experimental study, each preschool subject played alone, without any social interaction, for twenty minutes before he participated in a simple learning experiment. A control group of children were presented with the same learning problem but did not experience this kind of social deprivation. The reward for correct responses during learning was a social one: verbal approval by the experimenter.

The experimental (deprived) subjects were more responsive to this reward; that is, they learned faster than the control group did. Apparently, absence of social interaction—and the concomitant lack of gratification of dependency needs—leads to a greater need for attention and approval (dependence on others), thus increasing the reward value of verbal expressions of approval. Furthermore, children who are characteristically more dependent (according to observation of their behavior in nursery school) reacted more favorably to adult approval in the experimental situation. In this age group, approval by a woman experimenter was

* N. Feshbach and S. Feshback, "Children's Aggression," in Hartup, *The Young Child,* 2:298.

more effective for boys, whereas approval by a male experimenter was more effective for girls.

Another experimental study demonstrates even more clearly that deprivation of social contact and reassurance heightens a child's dependency. A female experimenter, while watching a group of nursery school children playing freely with toys, gave them a great deal of attention and affection, thus gratifying their dependency needs. Then, abruptly, she stopped talking to them, withdrawing her attention and nurturance, and refusing to answer their questions. In psychological terms, after gratifying the children's dependency needs for a period of time, she frustrated them. A control group of children received consistent dependency-need gratification; that is, the experimenter did not withdraw her affection and attention or frustrate their dependency needs. Later, while learning a task, the children in the frustrated group appeared to be much more highly motivated to seek praise by the experimenter—that is, to be nurtured and to have their dependency needs gratified—than the control group. Apparently, gratification of dependency needs followed by social deprivation enhanced their dependency motivation. This was particularly true for the girls.

As in the study reported above, boys who were ordinarily highly dependent reacted most strongly to this frustration; they became highly motivated to receive praise from the experimenter. Independent boys, however, were not so much affected by withdrawal of nurturance and attention. We may conclude that although deprivation of nurturance and warmth is likely to strengthen a young child's dependency needs at least temporarily, the intensity of his reactions will be conditioned by his personality structure and earlier experiences.

The Modification of Children's Personality Characteristics

The fact that children's behavior can be influenced significantly by situational factors is further evidence that the behavior patterns of young children are flexible and modifiable. Consequently, if they encounter new situations, particularly new social interactions, their personality structure and behavior may undergo radical modifications.

To illustrate, experiences with peers in school may foster self-confidence in a child who previously lacked this characteristic. A shy, sullen, and withdrawn child, the product of a harsh and restrictive home environment, may expand in a permissive nursery school with warm, understanding teachers, becoming lively, happy, and creative. Similarly, a boy who is unable to identify with a cold, unkind father may be retarded in the acquisition of sex-typed characteristics and interests. If he forms a strong friendship with a highly masculine boy, identification may then promote and accelerate the boy's sex-typing, compensating at least in part for earlier difficulties in this area.

On the other hand, unfortunate school or neighborhood experiences may undermine the beneficial effects of good parent-child relationships. For example, if his parents have been warm, gentle, and permissive, a child may enter school feeling secure, self-possessed, and confident. But if he is below average in intelligence or lacking in motivation to study, he may experience crushing failures in school and as a consequence become frustrated and aggressive. He may change from a socially outgoing and pleasant youngster into an unhappy, withdrawn, socially maladjusted one. In short, encountering new situations—particularly social relationships—may lead to major readjustments and significant alterations in a child's personality and behavior.

Simple applications of basic principles of social learning and reinforcement may produce dramatic modifications in behavior and personality characteristics. In one classic experiment, twelve nursery school children with immature reactions to failure (retreating, giving up easily, crying, sulking) were given special training designed to increase their perseverance and independence in solving difficult problems. A control group of twelve children who were only slightly immature received no special training. In the training, the experimenter met with each child a number of times, introducing him to problems and encouraging him to work them out independently. As training progressed, the problems became more complex and difficult, but the youngsters became more interested and gained continuously in independence. They requested less help and persevered longer in their attempts to solve the problems. Spontaneous comments showing self-confidence (for instance, "It's a hard problem but I'm getting better all the time") became more frequent.

After training, the control and experimental groups were given new difficult puzzles to solve. The trained group showed a significantly greater increase in independence than the controls and greater interest than they had shown originally, and they worked harder than they did before training. Crying, sulking, aggressive outbursts, and destruction occurred less frequently as reactions to difficult problems. Mature, independent responses, learned during the training, were apparently generalized to the new problems. The control group, however, did not show significant improvements in their attempts to solve difficult problems or in their reactions to frustration.

Nursery school teachers can create simple new situations that produce some behavior modifications. As we have seen, some children behave very aggressively in the permissive milieu of the nursery school. Nevertheless, slight changes in the teacher's response to aggression may produce some marked modifications in aggression, as the following study demonstrated. For two weeks, the experimenters, who were teachers in a nursery school, ignored children's aggression as much as possible and rewarded cooperative and peaceful behavior with attention and praise. Pupils' aggressive responses had been observed and rated for a week before the training period to determine their "base rate," and similar ratings were made again after the first week of the training period.

The simple manipulations of rewarding cooperation and ignoring (not rewarding) aggression were successful very soon, and apparently had some enduring effects. Acts of physical and verbal aggression decreased significantly in the second week of the experiment, while the number of cooperative acts increased. Some extremely aggressive boys became friendly and cooperative to a degree that could hardly have been anticipated before the training began. The source of these impressive changes was a simple manipulation of the environment, a simple application of basic principles of reinforcement learning.

Peers can be agents of behavior modification (and successful psychotherapists!) simply by serving as models of adaptive behavior. This was dramatically illustrated in the study of the "treatment" of a group of children of nursery school age who had dog phobias (excessive fear of dogs). They observed eight sessions of a four-year-old model playing with a dog and petting him. In each successive session, the model stayed with the dog for a longer period of time, interacting with him more intensively. A control group of children with equally severe phobias did not observe the model.

The day after the treatment series was completed, each child was observed as he met the dog again. Those who had observed the model approached the dog readily, petted him, and played with him. A month later these gains were still apparent, and friendly approach responses were generalized from the familiar dog to an unfamiliar one. The controls, however, were just as fearful as they had been previously and avoided the dog.

Experiments and observations such as these lead us to conclude that a young child's immature and maladaptive responses can be modified relatively readily. With a little fairly simple training, a child may acquire better ways of coping with frustration and become more independent, more persevering, calmer, less aggressive, more cooperative, and less fearful. Most significantly, the changes produced in the training situation are likely to generalize to other situations.

The Development of
Social Behavior

chapter six

Our discussion of personality development in Chapters 4 and 5 necessarily included some consideration of significant aspects of social behavior, because evaluations of children's personality are based largely on observations of their interactions with others. For example, we judge children to be highly aggressive if they attack or quarrel with peers frequently; domineering if they try to control or boss others; and dependent if they seek a great deal of aid or reassurance from other children or adults. In a sense, then, our discussion of the development of social interactions and the antecedents of individual differences in social behavior began in earlier sections of this volume that dealt with personality characteristics and attitudes.

In the present chapter our attention will be centered directly on the nature and characteristics of peer interactions, including friendship; on the structure of children's groups; on peer acceptance or popularity; on leadership; and on children's opinions and attitudes.

Psychologists can study children's social behavior and development by means of careful, naturalistic observation or using experimental methods. In *observation*, an investigator usually finds a good lookout station in a nursery school, playground, or meeting place and, usually using a time-sampling method, systematically records children's interactions. For example, if he were interested in aggressive behavior, he would note all instances of hitting others, destroying toys, and shouting at the teacher or other children. Or he could use a checklist with many aggression items and check the appropriate ones as various behaviors occurred. In *experiments* on the development of social behavior, he would put children in a specially contrived setting, observing and recording their reactions to the situation and to other children.

Social Behavior During the Preschool Years

We know very little about babies' social motivations or their relationships with peers—or if indeed babies have real social interactions at all. Infants evidently do react to peers, but their responses are not as clear or focused as their responses to adults. It is therefore extremely difficult to do research on the *beginnings* of social behavior. However, recently there have been some fascinating initial attempts to determine the nature of infants' social actions toward their peers.

In one ongoing short-term longitudinal study, babies are observed repeatedly (at four-week and six-week intervals) between the ages of twelve and twenty-four months. The setting is a very natural one, an informal play group. The baby is with his mother, a number of peers, strange adults (the mothers of his peers), and a few toys. Using three five-minute time samples—one at the beginning, one in the middle, and one at the end of the forty-five minute play session—observers record every instance of social contact, such as glances, looks, smiles, gestures, stretching out the arms, and vocalizing.

While only preliminary data based on a small sample are available so far, some of the results are extremely interesting and provocative. The vast majority of social responses at this age are very brief ones, three-quarters of them lasting less than thirty seconds. A large proportion of the social contacts are not real interactions; rather, one child initiates a social contact but generally elicits no response beyond a gaze or glance from the others. There is little change in the nature of social interactions during the second year. Children this age participate very little in real interactive play (staying close to another child while sharing a common toy), although there is a slight increase toward the end of the second year. Among the real interactions (social actions that elicit some reaction from another baby), the most frequent type involves disputes over toys and possessions. However, the investigator warns that a baby's behavior may be quite different from his intention, which cannot be assessed directly.

Despite the frequency of dispute and nonaffiliative behaviors, it would be highly misleading to take these data as indicating that the children we observed were mostly aggressive little beasts. To give just one instance of the observations that lead me to stress this point: in Playsession 5, a 17-month-old boy turns to the 18½-month-old girl, hits her shoulder, and then proceeds to repeatedly hit her back in a series lasting for 14 seconds. She turns and looks at him. He follows by another hit and a yank of hair. She again turns and gazes at him, while one of the mothers . . . touches the boy in restraint, another admonishes him to be gentle, and he is physically redirected away. In less than a minute the little girl turns to the little boy and offers him a toy. He accepts it, and both children divert to engage in other activities. In this sequence of two interactions, the adults' reactions clearly differ from the response achieved from the peer; the question of the nature of the initiator's intent and the recipient's interpretation of a behavior is obviously an important one.*

An infant may be more responsive when he is alone with one other infant than when he is with a group of others, as in the study discussed above. In one cross-sectional study, babies between six and twenty-five months of age were placed together in pairs in a playpen, and observed for four-minute periods. With increasing age, responses changed steadily from initial indifference toward the partner to social interest and co-operative play. Infants between six and eight months of age generally ignored each other, but there were a few rudimentary social contacts, such as looking, smiling, and grasping the partner. Babies between nine and thirteen months of age paid some attention to their partners, and conflicts occurred if one child attempted to snatch a toy from the other. Between fourteen and eighteen months, attention to the partner as an individual increased considerably, and, simultaneously, conflicts over toys decreased. In the last age period studied, between nineteen and twenty-five months, there were more social contacts—looking and smiling at the partner—and play became far more cooperative and friendly. In general, for children in the second year, being in a confined area with one other child is more conducive to sociability than a situation that includes many babies together in a large room. Nevertheless, social relationships during the second year are very limited.

Social development is markedly accelerated during the nursery school period, when the child's contacts with peers become more frequent and intense. In one well-known study, time samples of interactions in nursery

---

* W. C. Bronson, "Competence and the Growth of Personality," in *The Development of Competence in Early Childhood*, ed. J. S. Bruner and K. J. Connolly (New York: Academic Press, in press).

school were categorized according to a hierarchy of six increasingly mature and cooperative social responses: unoccupied behavior; solitary play (independent of other children); onlooker behavior (watching, but not playing with, others); parallel play (playing alongside, but not with, others); associative play (playing with others in joint projects, sharing materials); cooperative, organized play (each child making contributions to joint play).

With increasing age between two and five, children spend more time in more advanced types of social behavior (parallel, associative, and cooperative activity) and less time in relatively nonsocial activities such as idleness, solitary play, and onlooker behavior. The correlation between chronological age and social participation is substantial (.61). The most rudimentary form of social interaction, parallel play, is characteristic of two-year-olds, but relatively uncommon among children four or five years of age. The latter participate more in associative or cooperative play.

Many factors account for these shifts in social behavior. The increased physical and cognitive abilities that develop as the child becomes more mature enable him to participate in more complex, cooperative activities. Moreover, older children have experienced more rewards for outgoing and friendly responses, and at nursery school and on playgrounds cooperative, socially oriented responses bring further reinforcements; hence, these responses are more apt to be repeated. At the same time, inactivity and merely observing others are discouraged by parents and nursery school teachers, so these become weaker responses and tend to drop away.

PRESCHOOL FRIENDSHIPS

Between the ages of two and five, the number of conflicts and quarrels between children decreases steadily and friendly contacts become more prominent. During these years, children form their first friendships, usually with others of their own sex, although sex cleavage in social relationships is not as strong at this age as during middle childhood and preadolescence. Between the ages of two and three, the number of friends a child has tends to increase; after this age, closer attachments to a few particular friends develop. Nevertheless, preschool friendships are generally casual, unstable, and highly transient.

A socially oriented and responsive preschooler who seeks out companions has a variety of social experiences, some satisfying and some frustrating. Consequently, he may exhibit social responses that seem contradictory. For example, preschool friends tend to argue more frequently with each other than children who rarely associate with one another. Highly aggressive nursery school children are also very sympathetic with their classmates, responding readily to their distress. The child who grabs a toy from a playmate at one moment may rush to comfort a crying, unhappy child the next.

POPULARITY DURING PRESCHOOL

Popular children and leaders can be distinguished as early as the nursery school period. Some children are continually being sought out as playmates; others are consistently shunned and avoided by their nursery school classmates. The popularity status of a child can be assessed by observing his social participation directly, noting the number and nature of social contacts with his peers. Or *sociometric* questions can be used; the child is asked to name (or to choose from among the pictures of all the children in the school) the children in his class he likes best, wants to play with, wants to sit next to, dislikes, etc.

Popularity has been found to be significantly correlated with behavioral measures of friendliness (number of friendly approaches to others and participation in associative play) and with peers' perceptions of friendliness. Popular children are those who are much more likely than unpopular ones to give their peers social reinforcements (attention or approval, affection, indications of acceptance, imitation of another child, willing compliance with another's request) and they give these reinforcements to a greater number of children. As one might expect, aggressiveness is negatively correlated with popularity; popular children have relatively few fights with others, and they seldom attack or insult their peers. They also tend to be generally conforming and cooperative in their approach to nursery school routines, not because they are passive or overly compliant, but rather because they are willing "to modulate their own behavior and to make necessary compromises toward the peaceful and efficient operation of the group."*

Dependency is also related to peer acceptance, but in rather complicated ways. Emotional dependence on adults—for example, seeking attention, comfort, and support from teachers—is significantly negatively related to popularity. Peer-oriented dependency, on the other hand, is positively correlated. "A child's need or desire to seek help, affection, and support from his companions may actually enhance him in their

---

* S. G. Moore, "Correlates of Peer Acceptance in Nursery School Children," in *The Young Child: Reviews of Research*, ed. W. W. Hartup and N. L. Smothergil (Washington, D.C.: National Association for the Education of Young Children, 1967), p. 241.

eyes. Young children may be somewhat flattered at having a companion come to them for help, affection, and support."*

SOCIAL CONFLICTS

There are great individual differences in proneness to conflicts, but the average nursery school child between two and four years of age is involved in some sort of conflict every five minutes. Boys tend to participate in more conflicts and make more attacks, whereas girls tend to argue more. These sex differences are more pronounced among older nursery school children, reflecting their more firmly established sex-typing of behavior.

In general, the interactions of preschool youngsters are more characteristically cooperative and friendly than unfriendly, hostile, or competitive. Even the most highly aggressive preschool children actually make more friendly than aggressive responses. Aggressiveness, incidentally, tends to be a fairly stable characteristic; the frequency of a child's conflicts during nursery school is a reliable indicator of his proneness to conflict in kindergarten.

COMPETITION

Although social participation as well as associative and cooperative play increase during the preschool years, competition and rivalry also mount. On the average, two-year-olds are not competitive, but rivalry appears as early as the age of three or four. In one study, children were brought together in pairs and given a pile of blocks to play with. Each child was instructed to compete, to build something prettier or bigger than his companion. Those between the ages of four and six compete with considerable intensity, grabbing materials from each other, disregarding the other child's feelings and intentions, and refusing to give help or materials. By this age, competitive motives are strong enough to produce improvement in performance when a child is competing with someone else. As children advance in age, they become acutely aware of the culture's prevalent attitudes toward and consistent rewards for competition; hence, they adopt competitive values and motivations.

Boys compete more than girls, and lower-middle-class children are more competitive than those from the upper middle class. Highly competitive children often come from democratic, freedom-giving homes, but they are also likely to have histories of conflicts with siblings. During the

* Ibid., p. 244.

preschool period, competition and aggression appear to be relatively independent; that is, the most competitive children are not ordinarily the
most aggressive. Among older children and adults, these motives are
likely to be more closely associated.

Social Relationships in Middle Childhood

Social relationships during the school years are more extensive, more
intense, and more influential than those of the earlier years. While preschool friendships are generally casual and of short duration, the school
child's friends are likely to be important agents of socialization, having
direct and powerful impacts on his personality and social development.

From roughly ages seven to twelve, youngsters are strongly concerned
with their "gang," an informal group with a fairly rapid turnover in
membership. Later on, between the ages of ten and fourteen, more highly
structured groups with formal organization and membership requirements, such as Boy Scouts and Girl Scouts, become more salient, especially among middle-class children.

POPULARITY

The personality characteristics associated with popularity during
middle childhood parallel those associated with preschool popularity—
friendliness, sociability, outgoingness, sensitivity to the needs and feelings of other children, and enthusiasm. Emotional adjustment (relative
freedom from anxiety), acceptance of others, cooperativeness, and conformity to group standards are also positively correlated with popularity
during this period. The expression of inappropriate aggression—aggression that is immature, unprovoked, indirect, and insulting—is negatively
correlated with popularity, although, according to some studies, responding aggressively when provoked is associated with peer acceptance.

FRIENDSHIPS

In choosing friends, children between eight and adolescence generally
prefer members of their own sex. Between the ages of six and eight, sex
is ignored in play groupings, but at approximately eight, attitudes seem
to change and associations with members of the opposite sex decrease
sharply. By eleven or twelve boys and girls in our culture are almost
completely segregated from each other in play groups and in social gath-
erings. "This stage of segregation began with haughty aloofness, became
apparent contempt, and active hostility, and then changed to shy with-

drawal which seemed to mark the end of this period and the beginning of adolescent heterosexuality after puberty."*

The segregation of the sexes during these years is probably related to sex-typing and to cultural pressures on children to adopt sex-appropriate behavior. In our culture, many activities, interests, and attitudes are sex-typed by the age of nine. As social attitudes and values change— and they seem to be changing very rapidly at present—there will undoubtedly be less stress on stereotyped sex roles and patterns of behavior. However, among American children in the early 1970s there are striking sex differences in play, reading, movie and television preferences, and vocational choices and aspirations. Boys between the ages of eight and eleven are principally interested in playing active, vigorous, competitive games involving muscle skills and dexterity, while girls of this age generally engage in quieter, more sedentary activities. Occupational choices also reflect sex-typing, boys choosing such vocations as scientist or pilot and girls aspiring to activities such as teaching, nursing, or social work. Since peers of the same sex are more likely to have the same needs and interests, they are more likely to be more satisfying and rewarding friends.

Children's "best friends" are usually from their own neighborhood or classroom and have valued personality characteristics. When asked the reasons for choosing their friends, children in the second grade stress external factors—a nice home, good looks, having money to spend. Sixthgraders, however, emphasize personal characteristics such as friendliness, cheerfulness, and similarity of interests.

Pairs of friends (reciprocated friendships) tend to resemble each other in social maturity, chronological age, height, weight, general intelligence, and educational and occupational goals. Are friends chosen on the basis of *similarity* in personality characteristics, or do opposites attract? There is no clearcut answer to this question. Certainly, capable, friendly, energetic, responsive, outgoing, adventurous children are often attracted to each other, probably because they understand each other better and satisfy each other's needs. Other kinds of children are often attracted to those with these characteristics, but they are usually rejected.

One study yielded some evidence of *complementarity*—opposites attracting—in the reciprocal friendship choices of eighth-grade boys. For example, many attention-seeking boys had friends who were willing to share the limelight, and were supportive of them. Among the girls in this same study, there was no evidence of complementarity in friendship choices. Rather, mutual friends were alike on variables of outgoingness, concern with having a good time, and interest in social activity.

* E. H. Campbell, *The Social-Sex Development of Children*, Genetic Psychology Monographs, vol. 21, no. 4, (1939), p. 465.

The friendships of middle childhood are fairly unstable. Since interests fluctuate rapidly at this time, "old" friends may no longer provide the gratifications they provided a short time earlier, and consequently friendships may be terminated quickly and new friends substituted. With advancing age, interests become more crystallized; concomitantly, friendships are more stable and enduring.

Social Patterns of Adolescents

The social relationships of adolescents are more complex and have more ramifications than those of younger children. The adolescent's social situation is a particularly difficult one, since he lives simultaneously in two worlds, a children's and an adults', in a kind of marginal or overlapping status, not knowing where he belongs. All at once he has many new urgent, conflicting demands put on him: choosing a vocation; achieving some independence from his family; coping with strong, forbidden sexual impulses. Peers can be of inestimable value in helping the adolescent deal with his complex feelings, conflicts, and forbidden or suppressed feelings. Intimate adolescent friends feel free to discuss these matters openly and to criticize each other. Consequently, they may learn to modify behavior, tastes, and ideas without painful experiences of disapproval or rejection.

Since the adolescent has greater mobility than the younger child, his social world broadens and he can maintain friendships over a wider geographical area. Earlier, most of his peers and friends were from his own neighborhood and social-class group, but in high school he is likely to meet boys and girls from other parts of his community and from other ethnic and cultural groups. Furthermore, he is more open to new experiences and new ideas, more flexible, in his thinking. Hence, the adolescent has many opportunities to acquire new attitudes, customs, and value systems.

GROUP DYNAMICS OF ADOLESCENT GROUPS

A fascinating series of studies conducted by Musafer Sherif and his colleagues is the source of many insights into group formation, intergroup relations, intergroup tensions, and leadership during adolescence. The findings of these studies have important implications not just for understanding adolescents, but also for understanding group dynamics in general.

A group of middle-class white Protestant boys were taken to a summer camp and divided into two subgroups that were carefully matched in ability and personality characteristics. There was very little contact between the two groups during the five days of the study; they occupied separate cabins, and had their own programs of activities with very little adult leadership. Within this short period, clear hierarchical structures emerged in both groups. Leadership and "low man on the totem pole" positions crystallized early. Leaders tended to be highly intelligent, active, sociable, assertive and aggressive boys, although leadership and popularity were only slightly correlated.

Nor did it take long for each group to establish standards and norms. Each group adopted an identifying group nickname, and there was considerable "we-they" discussion. The group members themselves formulated rules, sanctions, and punishments, although these norms were flexible and modifiable as the interests and attitudes of group members changed.

> Emergent hierarchies and shared norms . . . maintain the existence of the group. It does not follow that children have a "natural" propensity for forming structured groups or that they need to share norms with peers in order to survive. Rather, it seems that the incentives and punishments arising from peer interaction itself produce these outcomes; these outcomes, in turn, serve to sustain the group.*

Using the same partially naturalistic, partially experimental techniques —that is, dividing a summer camp group into two separate groups—the investigators attempted to make each group a cohesive unit by forcing the members to cooperate in many daily activities, such as securing food and preparing and serving meals. It did not take long for the members of these groups to develop strong feelings of group belongingness. Once these feelings had been established, the investigators began to set up competition between the two groups. For example, they arranged competitive games and awarded prizes to the winning team. Under these conditions, tensions between the groups developed rapidly, and the investigators created situations to raise the level of these tensions. They arranged a party and contrived to have one group arrive some time before the other. By the time the second group arrived, the first group had eaten the best refreshments, leaving only the most unappetizing for their rivals. Understandably, hostile feelings increased, the boys called each other names, and they threw food, cups, and other objects, at one another.

The investigators then attempted to reduce the intergroup hostilities

---

* W. W. Hartup, "Peer Interaction and Social Organization," in *Carmichael's Manual of Child Psychology*, 3rd ed., ed. P. H. Mussen (New York: Wiley, 1970), 2:371.

by eliminating competitive conflict situations and encouraging simple noncompetitive contacts between groups—for example, watching movies together, eating in the same room, and playing in the same area. This attempt backfired, however; putting the groups in close proximity only served to increase their hostilities toward each other.

Only by getting members of the two groups to cooperate did the investigators succeed in reducing these hostilities. They formed an all-star baseball team that included members from both groups and played against a group of boys from a nearby town. The camp truck "unexpectedly" broke down and all the boys had to cooperate in repairing it so that they could go on a camping trip. After a number of these cooperative ventures, intergroup animosity was considerably reduced and friendships developed between members of the two different groups. In fact, they began to cooperate spontaneously in other situations, and evidences of hostility disappeared.

These investigations give us important information about the function of cooperation and competition in the development of in-group feelings and intergroup hostility. They also have some practical implications.

> If, for example, the membership of two hostile peer groups can be reshuffled and the newly formed groups induced to function with some common purpose, interpersonal hostility *within* each new group should diminish. Further, if two hostile groups combine to work cooperatively toward a superordinate goal, intergroup hostility should be reduced.*

Adolescent cliques and crowds.   Analyses of peer interactions suggest that there are two basic kinds of groups during adolescence: relatively large crowds and much smaller cliques (generally about one-third the size of the crowd). The crowd is essentially an association of cliques, although an individual may be a clique member but not a crowd member. A clique is generally a small group that includes the individual's best friends and a few other adolescents, usually not more than six or seven. This permits and encourages a higher degree of intimacy and group cohesion, and consequently fosters discussion of basic needs, conflicts, feelings, and ideas. Larger, more organized social activities such as parties are more likely to be crowd functions. Dexter Dunphy, a sociologist who has studied adolescent peer groups in depth, notes that structural changes develop in five stages.

"*Stage 1:* Persistence of the preadolescent same-sex cliques into the adolescent period.

Stage 2: Same-sex cliques begin to participate in heterosexual action —often of a superficially antagonistic sort—but these interactions occur

---

* Ibid., p. 372.

only in the security of the group setting where the individual is supported by close friends of his own sex.

Stage 3: High-status members of girl cliques begin to interact on an individual basis with high-status members of boy cliques. This makes the transition to heterosexual cliques while each individual still maintains membership in his same-sex clique.

Stage 4: Reorganization of same-sex cliques and the formation of new heterosexual crowds, made up of heterosexual cliques in close association.

Stage 5: The slow disintegration of the crowd and the formation of cliques consisting of couples who are going steady or engaged."*

Crowd and clique membership in high school is strongly influenced by factors such as social class, educational aspiration (planning to go to college or not), ethnic background, neighborhood, common interests and hobbies, social and personal maturity, and degree of heterosexual interest. Boys' groups are somewhat more democratic and flexible than girls' groups, and athletic skills and overall sociability are more critical considerations.

ADOLESCENT FRIENDSHIPS

As we noted earlier, adolescents in our culture often experience doubts, anxieties, and strong resentments. They desperately need friends whom they can trust completely, with whom they can share their complex feelings, conflicts, and secrets without fear of misunderstanding or rejection. For these reasons, adolescent friendships are typically more intimate, more honest and open, and involve more intense feelings than those of earlier periods. Consequently, they contribute more to the individual's development.

> The particular advantage of the adolescent friendship is that it offers a climate for growth and self-knowledge that the family is not equipped to offer, and that very few persons can provide for themselves. Friendship engages, discharges, cultivates, and transforms the most acute passions of the adolescent, and so allows the youngster to confront and master them. Because it carries so much of the burden of adolescent growth, friendship acquires at this time a pertinence and intensity it has never had before nor (in many cases) will ever have again.†

The nature of friendship relationships changes during the period of

---

* D. C. Dunphy, "The Social Structure of Urban Adolescent Peer Groups," *Sociometry* 26 (1963):238.

† E. Douvan and J. Adelson, *The Adolescent Experience* (New York: John Wiley, 1966), p. 174.

adolescence. Early adolescent friendships are relatively more superficial, involving doing favors for each other, sharing activities, and simply getting along well. By mid-adolescence, relationships are "mutual, inter-active, emotionally interdependent; the personality of the other and the other's response to the self become the central themes of friendship."* During this period, adolescents reveal a distinctive talent for friendship. More than at earlier or later ages, the individual is flexible and ready to change—and convinced that by conscious, deliberate effort he *can* change.

Understandably then, the major criteria used in selecting friends are loyalty, understanding, trustworthiness, respect for confidences, and sup-portiveness in emotional crises. Mutual friends are likely to resemble each other in such personality and social characteristics as age, intelli-gence, socioeconomic status, shared interests, and career goals. While friendships may sometimes involve complementarity—an extroverted adolescent girl may have a shy, inhibited friend—similarities are gen-erally more prominent than differences.

In later adolescence, as heterosexual relationships develop, there is less exclusive reliance on friends of the same sex. Sharing confidences with someone is still important, but there is a greater emphasis on friends' personality and talents and on how interesting and stimulating he or she is. More mature friendship relationships involve a great degree of toler-ance for individual differences, and as the adolescent begins to develop a firm sense of ego identity he becomes less intensely dependent on identification with close friends.

HETEROSEXUAL RELATIONS DURING
ADOLESCENCE

During the junior high school years, boys and girls are at distinctly different levels of biological and social maturity. Some girls are interested in boys, but their male contemporaries do not generally reciprocate their interest. At this age, girls are much more concerned with social life and heterosexual behavior than boys are.

All this changes by about the sophomore year of high school, when boys begin to catch up with girls in maturity and in interest in the oppo-site sex. Boys' and girls' interests now begin to complement each other, and they pay more attention to one another. In early adolescence, during the period of initial heterosexual relationships, the individual is still pretty much involved in finding himself, in achieving ego identity. Be-cause he is still relatively preoccupied with himself and his own problems

---

* Ibid., p. 188.

and therefore unlikely to become deeply emotionally involved with someone of the opposite sex,

> there is usually a superficial "game-like" quality to heterosexual inter-
> actions. At this juncture, heterosexual group activities are common and
> may serve a useful function—providing the security of having familiar
> same-sex peers present. [These activities offer graduated] opportunities
> to learn ways of relating to opposite-sex peers, and insuring that one
> will not have to cope with being alone in a dating context with an
> opposite-sex peer for prolonged periods before one is prepared to.*

Gradually, with greater experience with heterosexual cliques, increased
personal maturity, and greater self-confidence, heterosexual relations
become more mature. When the adolescent has achieved a clearer sense
of himself, generally in late adolescence, he can form genuine relationships with others. These will be based not only on sexual attraction, but
on shared trust and confidence together with concern about the interests
and well-being of the other person.

Dating can serve a number of useful social functions, including the
further development of social and interpersonal skills, discovering and
testing one's own identity, and providing occasions for sexual experimentation and discovery. Most importantly, dating permits the development of an understanding of reciprocal relationships of love, trust, and
mutual concern between opposite-sex peers.

Compared with other cultures, American culture has traditionally been
rather restrictive about sexual expression among children and adolescents.
However, our standards of sexual morality and sexual behavior appear
to be changing rapidly. Today's adolescents believe that a new sexual
morality is developing, but they do not view the change as a lowering of
morals. Rather, they see their attitudes and approaches as more honest
and open than those of earlier generations.

Most older adolescents and young people consider premarital intercourse acceptable when the couple is engaged, going steady, or has an
understanding about getting married. Promiscuity is not sanctioned; the
vast majority disapprove of premarital sexual relations between people
who are merely "casually attracted" or "good friends." Furthermore,
among adolescents the younger ones are the more conservative; permissive attitudes toward premarital sexual relationships become more prevalent with increasing age.

Changes in sexual behavior have also been well-documented. While
the incidence of masturbation by male and female adolescents has not
changed in the past few decades, there has been a change in attitudes

* J. J. Conger, *Adolescents and Youth: Psychological Development in a Changing World* (New York: Harper & Row, in press).

about the practice—greater objectivity, reduced anxiety and guilt. The percentage of college students who engage in premarital sexual intercourse has increased significantly over the same period. According to Alfred Kinsey's data, collected in the middle and late 1940s, the rate of incidence of premarital sex among the college-educated was 49 percent for males and 25 percent for females. In the early 1970s, the incidence was 82 percent for men and 56 percent for women. These of course are overall statistics, and there are wide differences among groups within the population. For example, the rate of incidence among college students is highest in eastern and West Coast colleges and among those attending "elite" private colleges and universities; it is lowest among those attending midwestern and church-related institutions. Politically liberal students tend to be more permissive with respect to sexual behavior, while those who are more conservative politically are also more conservative in their sexual attitudes and behavior.

ADOLESCENT VALUES AND BELIEFS

We have heard a great deal in recent years about adolescence and youth being "in revolt" and creating a "counterculture." In the light of the evidence, this seems to be a gross exaggeration of the facts. Certainly many adolescents have opinions, attitudes, and values that are significantly different from those of their parents. In addition, substantial, highly visible minorities of high school and college students are vocal and articulate about their profound disillusionment with our society, which they regard as corrupt, unjust, violent, hypocritical, cruel, impersonal, superficial, and overly competitive. Nevertheless, the average adolescent's values are much more traditional than newspaper and TV reports have led us to believe.

Evidence of this comes from a number of excellent investigations of the attitudes, beliefs, and opinions of nationwide, representative samples of adolescents. In one extensive study, hundreds of college and noncollege youths between seventeen and twenty-three years of age, and many of their parents, were interviewed and responded to questionnaires about individual initiative, self-reliance, property rights, law and order and political parties. For example, they were asked to indicate whether they agreed or disagreed with statements such as, "Hard work will always pay off"; "Belonging to some organized religion is important in a person's life"; "Competition encourages excellence"; and "Society needs some legally based authority in order to prevent chaos."

The vast majority of the subjects expressed agreement with traditional values in all areas, although the degree of agreement varied. Thus, there was least agreement on the importance of religion in a person's life (42 percent of college youth and 71 percent of noncollege youth agreed with the statement about the importance of religion) and greatest agreement on the need for "some legally based authority in order to prevent chaos" (92 percent of college youth and 94 percent of noncollege youth agreed with this statement). The differences between parents and youths on these issues were not large. In general, the noncollege population was more accepting of traditional points of view.

Although the majority of adolescents accept traditional values, many are dissatisfied with society and its major institutions. In the national study we have been discussing, the subjects were asked whether they felt changes were needed—and if so, how much—in big business, the military, the universities, trade unions, political parties, and the mass media. A substantial majority of the subjects expressed the belief that most of our social institutions are in need of at least "moderate" change, but less than 7 percent felt that any of these institutions should be "done away with." Only one in five young people felt that "no substantial change" was needed, and a majority agreed that "fundamental reform" in political parties was desirable.

Although only a minority of youth are militant activists on social and political issues, most appear to have greater concern than their parents do (or than their parents did as adolescents) with racial and socioeconomic discrimination, preservation of the environment, and the need for improved education. Compared with their parents, adolescents are much more likely to perceive discrimination against minorities and to favor increased school integration and having minority-group members as neighbors. "In their attitudes, most adolescents seem to be reflecting flexibility, tolerance, and lack of prejudice as much as, or more than, crusading zeal."*

What is perhaps most impressive is youth's widespread concern with humanitarian values and their pervasive desire to help create a world in which there is more true friendship, love, and kindness, greater individual freedom, and equality of opportunity for everyone.

> In brief, the average contemporary adolescent appears to be relatively more ready than his more self-conscious predecessors of earlier generations to put into practice a philosophy of "live and let live" and a pragmatic idealism. More than earlier generations, he appears to be a sophisticated and critical exponent of the art of the possible—not illusioned, but not disillusioned either.†

*Conger, *Adolescents and Youth.*
† Ibid.

Developmental Psychology and Human Welfare

Most psychologists share youth's concern with the human condition and with the improvement of society; they would like to contribute to the task of making this a better world to live in. Developmental psychology should play a significant role in achieving this goal. Many of society's problems have their roots in *individuals'* psychological development and early socialization. Investigations of the psychological antecedents of social problems yield information that has implications for eliminating or alleviating these problems. For example, as we learned earlier, developmental psychologists have discovered that children's cognitive deficiencies are in large part the products of extremely unstimulating environmental experiences in infancy and early childhood (see pp. 64–66). These findings are very useful in formulating programs of positive social actions—specifically, intensive programs to stimulate early cognitive development among disadvantaged children; some of these programs have proven to be very effective (see pp. 44–46).

As another example, consider again a social problem we discussed briefly on pages 76–77, juvenile delinquency. Well-designed studies of delinquents and matched controls demonstrate that poor parent-child relationships and parental rejection, physical punishment, and erratic discipline are major antecedent factors in juvenile delinquency. Most delinquents feel rejected by their parents, deprived, insecure, jealous of their siblings, uncomfortable about family tensions and parental misconduct, and thwarted in their needs for independence and self-expression. Delinquents do not readily identify with their parents, and partly for this reason they may fail to acquire acceptable patterns of social behavior. In brief, their delinquency may be viewed as the result of certain kinds of social learning and socialization experiences that lead them to behave in ways detrimental to their own and others' welfare and happiness.

Again, however, research findings allow us to sound an optimistic note. Delinquent behavior, like other maladaptive behavior, does not develop inevitably, and if it does develop it is not necessarily fixed and immutable. Like most other forms of maladjustment, delinquency consists of acquired—not biologically determined—patterns of responses, and these are modifiable. The findings about the childhood antecedents of delinquency may be useful in developing psychological, social welfare, and educational programs to aid parents in establishing better relationships with their children. At the same time, delinquents (and potential delinquents) must be helped to learn more adequate ways of handling their personal problems.

Racial prejudice is another social problem that has been studied developmentally. Anti–minority-group attitudes may be manifested as early as nursery school or kindergarten and often stem from personality structure, which in turn has its roots in the child's early socialization. Mothers of prejudiced, intolerant children are inclined to be highly critical, rigid, authoritarian, and controlling in their disciplinary practices. By contrast, mothers of unprejudiced children tend to be more permissive, affectionate, and wise in handling their children. In discussing their parents, tolerant youngsters frequently mention affection, cooperation, and companionship, whereas young bigots describe their parents as lacking in affection, stern, harsh, and punitive. As might be anticipated, therefore, prejudiced children have more narrow and rigid personalities, tend to think categorically in terms of "good and bad" or "strong and weak," and are intolerant of behavior that does not conform to conventional standards. They tend to accept uncritically the approved values of the groups they identify with.

Prejudiced children are basically frightened and frustrated; superficially they conform to authority, but they harbor deep-seated feelings of hostility and destructiveness. They admire all that is strong, tough, and powerful, but fear weakness in themselves. Characteristically, a prejudiced child lacks confidence in himself; is distrustful, uneasy, and insecure in social relationships; and feels discontented about his current status. When he feels frustrated—as he often does—he blames others, turning his aggression outward and displacing it onto others whom he sees as weak. In the not-too-distant past, minority groups were available and approved targets for displaced hostility, for race prejudice was a socially sanctioned form of expression of hostility. Now, fortunately, times have changed, and in a large portion of the population, particularly among adolescents and youth, prejudice against minority groups is not acceptable; minority groups are no longer approved targets of displaced aggression. And, as we have seen, prejudiced people conform to authority, including the authority of their own peer groups. This means that in conformity with their group, adolescents will not use prejudice against minorities—at least in its overt manifestations—as a way of displacing their deep-seated hostilities. This itself may result in substantial reduction in prejudices.

Are there more positive approaches to reducing or eliminating minority-group prejudices? Will such procedures as integration of schools be effective? Unfortunately, definitive answers to these questions are not yet available. But two relevant studies suggest that the tentative answer is positive.

In one intensive study, five black and five white children between two-and-one-half and three-and-one-half years of age in an integrated nursery school were observed systematically for over fifteen hours. The children had previously lived in segregated neighborhoods and had no experience with children of other races. During the first few weeks of school, racial characteristics seemed to have nothing to do with the children's activities or play; they spent most of their time exploring their new surroundings and playing spontaneously.

After the first few weeks, however, some children showed awareness of racial characteristics; some made positive statements, others negative ones. For example, one white child said to a black one, "I don't like the color of your skin." In spite of this, there was little evidence of strong rejection of black children by whites, and the integration was soon effective in overcoming manifest prejudices. By the middle of the school year, children no longer commented about race or racial differences, nor were their social roles or play behavior determined by racial-group membership. Instead, the relationships between children depended on the degree to which they satisfied each other's needs. Children played as long, and with as much satisfaction, with children of the other race as with children of their own race.

At this early age, race prejudice can be overcome readily and integration achieved without major problems. Early integration is probably the most complete and effective.

Under favorable circumstances, even brief interracial contacts can be effective in reducing children's prejudices. The subjects of one study of this phenomenon were children from low-income families in southern states attending an interracial camp where they were assigned to integrated cabins. The authority of the counselors supported the rules of the camp prescribing equal status for all in all activities. Two weeks of living together in an integrated setting produced no major shifts in long-standing racial attitudes, but the youngsters made significant adjustments rapidly. Judging from their overt behavior, the children accepted and conformed with the equalitarian philosophy of the camp, playing and working together happily and with little friction. When asked to name their best friends in their cabins, white children at first tended to select other whites, but this tendency decreased significantly by the end of the camp period. In general, the children enjoyed the interracial experience, over 75 percent of them expressing the wish that the camp period could be extended. The investigators felt that the consistent expectation of equality—conveyed by a racially integrated adult culture (the counselors) and expressed in the leaders' unprejudiced behavior—set the tone of the camp and thus produced positive results. Nevertheless, the investigators caution that this brief experience of integration "should probably be viewed not as completing the process of change in intergroup relations but as providing the necessary first steps in a long-term process of re-organizing beliefs and feelings."*

This study was completed in the late 1950s, before nationwide integration efforts were in full swing. Today the culture more vigorously encourages equalitarian, unprejudiced attitudes—and authorities strongly condemn prejudice—and we may therefore expect such efforts at integration to have even more striking, meaningful, and enduring results.

THE INVESTIGATION OF
POSITIVE SOCIAL BEHAVIOR

For many social and historical reasons, most of the research efforts in the field of child psychology in the past have been focused on socially undesirable behaviors and maladjustments such as aggression, competition, delinquency, and prejudice. As we have seen, knowledge of the psychological roots of such problems can be used in attempting to eliminate or ameliorate them.

Recently there has been an incipient but significant movement toward the investigation of the antecedents of positive, socially desirable behavior. The methods of developmental psychology are potentially useful for discovering the antecedents of such characteristics as personal happiness, competence, emotional maturity, creativity, tolerance, altruism, humanitarian values, kindness, and motivation to contribute to the general welfare. We reviewed a number of such studies earlier in this book. For example, we discussed the provocative study of the effects of authoritative parental treatment on the development of competence, self-reliance, and independence (see pp. 69–71). We also reviewed studies that demonstrate that observation of fearless peer models may lead to the reduction of children's fearful, maladaptive behavior (see pp. 88–89). Observation of models who behave generously may also foster altruism and generosity. Children playing a game with an adult observed him depositing some of his "winnings" in a charity box that stood prominently nearby; other children, the controls, did not observe him doing this. Not one child in the control condition contributed to the charity box; among those who observed the altruistic model, 63 percent contributed while the model was present, and more impressively, 50 percent also con-

* M. R. Yarrow, J. D. Campbell, and L. F. Yarrow, "Interpersonal Dynamics in Racial Integration," in *Readings in Social Psychology*, ed. E. E. Maccoby, T. M. Newcomb, and E. L. Hartley (New York: Holt, Rinehart and Winston, 1958), p. 635.

tributed in the model's absence, in a situation where no one would know whether the child had done so or not. Clearly, then, observation of an altruistic model facilitates altruism and charitability.

Other recent research gives us further important information about the antecedents and development of altruism. Positive relationships with parents who are models of selfless, prosocial behavior predispose children to altruistic behavior. In one investigation, nursery school boys were given some candy which they could either keep for themselves or divide among themselves and two of their friends. In subsequent doll play, generous boys (those who donated a substantial number of candies to others) portrayed their fathers as warmer, more giving, and more nurturant than boys who were not generous. Apparently, the generous boys identified with fathers who were themselves generous—at least in the child's perception.

The same conclusion emerges from an interesting study of two groups of student civil rights workers. One group, the *partially committed*, were occasional activists, limiting their participation in civil rights work to one or two freedom rides without giving up other activities; the other group, the *fully committed*, had been active participants in many civil rights actions for a year or longer and had given up a great deal to participate in these activities. Investigation of the family backgrounds of these two groups of young people showed that the parents of the fully committed were prosocial activists in their own youth, participating as volunteers in the Second World War, the Spanish Civil War, or religious education. In addition, the fully committed altruists maintained positive, cordial, warm, and respecting relationships with their parents. By contrast, the parents of the partially committed youth were mostly verbal supporters of altruism and moral behavior rather than activists. Many of their parents preached one thing and practiced another. In describing their parents, the partially committed civil rights workers were negative or ambivalent, often describing their relationships as hostile, cool, and avoidant. The contrast in the backgrounds of the two groups of students provides further evidence that long-term positive relationships with altruistic models is conducive to altruistic behavior.

Success in an undertaking leads to positive feelings, and such feelings also promote generosity and altruism. In a series of experiments, children experienced success, failure, or a neutral outcome in a game and were subsequently given an opportunity to contribute money to purchase toys for "children who have no toys." More of those who were successful in the games, and thus presumably had more positive feelings, contributed money, and they contributed greater amounts than children who failed or had a neutral outcome.

Finally, research data show that practice is much more important than preaching in the development of altruism. In one experimental setting, in the presence of the child subjects an adult behaved altruistically or greedily while at the same time preaching the opposite (with statements of the sort parents use with their children: "It is good to give to poor children"; "Be sure that you have enough before you consider others"; etc.). The results were very clearcut:

> Regardless of the variation employed, these experiments have produced one consistent outcome: moral preachings have less effect on behavior than moral practices.
> If the model behaves charitably, so will the child—even if the model has preached greed. And conversely, if the model preaches charity, but practices greed, the child will follow the model's behavior and will not contribute to the charity. Behavior in the prosocial area is mainly influenced by behavior, not by words.*

These findings on altruism are important in themselves; but even more significantly, the studies are models of the kind of research that is urgently needed if we are to understand the antecedents of positive social behavior. Without such understanding, we cannot develop methods of facilitating the adoption of such behavior. Happily, the movement toward more studies of positive social behavior is gaining considerable momentum, and in the near future our knowledge of prosocial behavior will be greatly expanded.

---

* D. Rosenhan, "Prosocial Behavior of Children," in *The Young Child: Reviews of Research*, ed. W. W. Hartup (Washington, D.C.: National Association for the Education of Young Children, 1972), 2:354.

Index